Dedication

This book is dedicated to all the artists, in every field, who embrace their hardships, including them as their inspiration for creative works. This requires a trust in something beyond themselves.

Jan Stirling

TED HARRISON'S RAINBOW ROAD

AUSTIN MACAULEY PUBLISHERS™

LONDON • CAMBRIDGE • NEW YORK • SHARJAH

A CIP catalogue record for this title is available from the British Library.

ISBN 9781788789875 (Paperback)
ISBN 9781788789882 (Hardback)
ISBN 9781788789899 (E-Book)

www.austinmacauley.com

First Published (2018)
Austin Macauley Publishers Ltd™
25 Canada Square
Canary Wharf
London
E14 5LQ

Acknowledgements

With love and appreciation for my long list of creative friends and family that have encouraged me along the way. With special mention of my musician uncle, Jim Maben, and, of course, Ted Harrison, who continues to nudge me from beyond.

Rainbow Road

Life is a Rainbow Road, multi-coloured with the most brilliant hues contrasting with the darkest tones. It is illuminated by the light of success and rutted by the tracks of failure. Tears of sadness and joy wash its surface while the clouds of doubt and insecurity dapple its course. As we traverse this highway, we can reach the highest pinnacle or descend to the darkest valleys.

Finally, when the end of the road is in sight, we may cast our eyes to the distant horizon where everything began and say with conviction, "That sure was one hell of a journey."

Written by Ted Harrison, given to Barry Bergh and donated to this book.

Cattle Point

We sat in my Honda down at Cattle Point, sipping from small bottles of champagne and gazing at the crashing waves in front of us. The wind buffeted the car, the dark sky was menacing, but we were cozy and comfortable, not feeling a need to talk. The occasional squeeze of our clasped hands expressed our delight. *There's nowhere else I'd rather be,* I thought, with surprise.

Once again, I was spending my Friday night with an eighty-two-year-old man. I had stopped trying to analyze or compartmentalize our relationship. Ted Harrison and I just were. We had met two years earlier when I was a member of the Rotary Club and then met again a year later, when I was going through a heart-breaking divorce and he was going through the more significant process of paring his worldly possessions to fit in a small apartment in a retirement home. Relinquishing symbols of freedom such as his piano, his huge book and art collections, and his lovely home and furniture must have been a devastating experience, but Ted had taken it in stride. He enjoyed his fellow residents at Carlton House and the delicious food they shared in the dining room. His tablemates were inspired by his enthusiasm and wicked wit, and often Ted would break into song and get them all to join in.

Although Ted Harrison was a famous Canadian artist, it was not his art that first attracted me to him. It was his liberated thinking, his compassion for the human spirit, his disgust of triteness and his silly sense of humour which resonated with my own. I could laugh and be myself with this man. I never felt judged, and always felt respected and loved.

To top it off, when he found out how lost I was as I struggled with being single, he phoned me almost every night to ask how I was doing. I had never spent time with such a considerate man in my life. Even when he went to Toronto to see friends and put on an art show, he called me. Our first date had been as dining guests at the elegant home of the Lieutenant Governor of B.C., when Ted had been honoured as an Order of B.C. recipient. I had often played piano there and even played at his ceremony in the afternoon, but to be dressed formally and seated around the large carved table in the dining room in the evening was a whole new level of experience.

"Isn't this lovely," enthused Ted. "I haven't had champagne in years. You know, I used to bring Maggie down here all the time."

I just smiled. I knew Maggie was one of the beloved dogs he used to own. I found it interesting that he spoke of Maggie more often than his family. It was getting chilly so I put my bottle in the cup holder and started the car. Soon, we were at my rental house, which fortunately was one level. Ted slowly made his way from the carport to the kitchen, while he leaned on his cane. We walked through to the living room and he plunked himself down on the old blue La-Z-Boy that came with the house. I had moved there the year before, from the home my ex-husband and I shared for eighteen years.

Ted looked around at the art work, the grand piano, and the stack of books.

"What a joy to be in a real home. I think I'll get another one – just a small one – and another dog."

I agreed as I always did. "Ted, I'm going to go finish cooking."

I put my favourite mellow jazz radio station on, without commercials, to give us some background ambiance and then handed him a couple of local artsy magazines.

"What else have you got to read?" asked Ted.

"I'm wondering if this would be of interest," I said. "My uncle just sent it to me. It's of some of his memories. I wish you could meet him. You're both about the same age and he's had a wonderful musical career in Toronto. He's funny and smart, and I'm sure you'd both get along. He was my inspiration and gave me my first piano when I was six."

"I'd love to read that," said Ted.

I left Ted with the stapled sheaf of papers, to stir-fry onions, garlic, snow peas and prawns. I wasn't a particularly good cook but we both preferred eating in a quiet home to a noisy restaurant. I knew if I put some curry spices in the coconut sauce, he would be happy. I could hear him chuckling in the living room. I hummed to myself as I moved around the kitchen. When the rice cooker indicated the rice was ready, I went to get him.

"Hey, Ted. Almost ready. What would you like to drink?"

"Red wine."

"With curry? You're as bad as me. Can you get yourself to the table while I dish up?" I pushed the footrest down and handed him his cane.

After squeezing lemon and snipping some cilantro onto each plate, I brought the food and wine to the dining room. Ted was already sitting with his napkin tucked into his collar, covering his front.

"It smells heavenly," said Ted. Without ceremony, he picked up a prawn and sucked the fresh meat from the tail. "How I love these little creatures." I was used to Ted concentrating on eating rather than talking so I relaxed and dug in. Then Ted said, "I really got a kick out of your uncle's writings. I can see why you love him. He pokes fun at himself and doesn't take himself too seriously. It sounds like he was pretty successful. He mentioned conducting a choir at the Roy Thompson Hall. Have you been to that lovely place? I went to see my friend, Gloria, play piano there a few years ago."

"I was in Toronto when he had his concert there. We have so many relatives, we took up two rows of seats. He and my mom come from a family of seven kids."

"Is one of them the painter that did these watercolours? Nice loose technique and he captures the fall colours."

"No, that's Uncle Bill, her sister's husband. I'm close with that family. They let me live with them now and then, when I was a teenager, even though they had five kids. They knew I had a rather tense home-life."

"I've met your mother and I can imagine what you must have gone through with her. And you continue to from afar. Thank God you're three thousand miles away."

"But I still let her push my buttons," I said. "I wish I could let it all go. I guess I still long to feel I'm loved as I am. I wish we could just be ourselves."

Ted pushed his plate aside and had a sip from his wine. "Yes, that shouldn't be asking too much. Are you still seeing that character that drives flowers across the country in a big rig? I can't believe there's money in that. What does that say about our crazy world?"

"They can't grow flowers like that in Alberta, I guess. Artie's on the road four days of the week, driving to Edmonton and Calgary, and back, so we're just getting to know each other. It's more like a long-distance relationship."

"I can't believe you went with him on one of those excursions."

"You know how I love an adventure. It was a fast way to get to know each other. And even though he was on a tight schedule, he'd stop so I could swim in lakes or take pictures and one night outside of Lytton, we camped on the Thompson River. I don't know how he got the truck down that gravel path but we had a fire, and smokies and wine. I'd only known him two weeks but it felt like we'd known each other in another life."

"What are smokies?"

"They're like hot dogs you put on a stick over the fire."

"I thought you didn't like that kind of food."

"Everything has its place Ted. Not a lot of options in that scenario."

"I would think long distance relationships can be very exciting."

"Tell me about it. That's how I ended up marrying both of my husbands. I was living in Vancouver when I started dating Ray. I should have stayed there." I sat for a moment, reviewing mistakes I had made in my life.

"Ah, but then you would have missed meeting me," said Ted, interrupting my depressing thoughts.

I grinned. "That would have been the biggest pity of all." I sipped my wine, appreciating the cheap Argentinian Malbec. "Ted, thanks for bringing me back to the positives."

"The what?"

"You don't let me dwell on the 'shoulda wouldas'."

"The what?"

"What I mean is, you don't seem to dwell on the negatives in your life. And you've had a fair number of them yourself."

"It helped to die when I had dysentery at the RAF clinic in India. Eight of the nine in the ward did die. I was the ninth but I returned."

"You mean you went to the other side? Tell me more; I love that stuff!"

"First, would you mind getting me a few more prawns and vegetables?"

As soon as I put his plate down, he lifted a prawn with his fingers and continued with his story.

"I floated above my gaunt body; the pain was gone and I was headed for a white light that was most compelling. I looked back and saw myself lying there but I also saw a friend of mine who had ridden his bike many miles to come and see me. He was standing at the foot of my bed calling me. Because of him, I chose to come back."

"Can you give me any details? Like smells, sounds, feelings?"

Ted chewed thoughtfully. "Not really. I just got a clear feeling that I had plenty to contribute, and I should get on with it. After recovering, I kept thinking about it for years. Although I had a family and a teaching career, and we lived in interesting places, I would often wonder what I should be doing with my artwork. I was a hard worker but I didn't feel I was doing anything special. However, it's probably what gave me the courage to extend myself and take jobs in two opposite ends of the world – New Zealand and the Yukon. And from those places and from teaching young people, I began to express my art in a new way. I wanted people to see the world as a bright place so I decided I would use vibrant colours. And since there are no straight lines in Nature, I modified my style accordingly."

"I've read a few books about people who died and came back again. One was written by a brain surgeon so he was very believable because he understood what was going on physically when he died and he described in gripping detail what he encountered on the other side. He realized that we are all connected to each other – to trees, animals, everything. Sounds like you might have had something similar happen."

"Unfortunately, I can't remember exactly what happened. All I know is that after that experience, I lost my fear and was able to trust my intuition."

"When you started painting differently, did people criticize you for changing your style?"

"Of course – it was so pared down and simple, they would say that any kid could copy it. I ignored it all. Just kept enjoying painting big skies, and animals and people with vivid colours."

"That's what Herbie Hancock says about creativity."

"Who?"

"An outstanding pianist. He says, 'just like a car barrelling through space against resistance – any new idea will meet opposition.' Every single one of Herbie's winning recordings is different from the last. He's a Buddhist so he says things like 'Beware of ego; creativity cannot flow when only the ego is served'."

"I'd be a Buddhist too if I had to be something, but fortunately I don't." Ted put his serviette on the table. "Wonderful meal, Pet. Thank you so much. May I go to my chair? I think I'm ready for us to write about Indian food. I'd like to think about that country."

"Sure," I said, picking up the plates. "I'll just put these in the sink and put the kettle on."

The previous year, I had started jotting down, as quickly as possible, Ted's thoughts on particular subjects. I had been struck by his gift with language and his fearlessness in trusting the words to come out seamlessly. My interest in musical improvisation had expanded to conversation, thanks to him. Because I would go home and type my scribbled notes, we now had several short, unedited essays, or poems, as we often called them.

By the time he was settled, I was across from him with a pad of paper and pen, while he spoke. Although his pace was slow, I was glad I could remember some of the symbols from the shorthand course I had taken years before.

Indian Food

When I approached India by sea, from a ten-mile distance, the wind was blowing softly from the land and I could smell the distinct smell of India. It was like eating curry in an outhouse – a subtle blend of exotic scents. Then, when I landed, the outhouse disappeared and the curry pervaded the air. The whole place is akin to a curry puff.

Open-air kitchens were frying, boiling, steaming and otherwise making foods much tastier than the plain meat and vegetables I was used to. There was also the strange scent of hookah pipes, whose owners sat placidly puffing their way into a state of nirvana. Their little bowls bubbled with each puff and the smoke was exhaled to mingle with all the other smells associated with the city. Perhaps, for centuries, these distinct scents have been a trademark of the East. One can walk down a street in the west and never smell anything cooking because boiled eggs don't give off a scent. But in the East, there is such a subtle series of aromas that invade the nostrils and raise the appetite. Then the dish we sit down to becomes a real adventure.

People grab the rice with the right hand and mop up gravy and chopped meat with skill and alacrity. The food is then pressed into wide-open mouths followed by a cacophony of belching, which proves to the cook that the food is being thoroughly enjoyed. A good belch is a compliment to the chef, whereas in the West it is considered ill-mannered. A meal in the East can last well over an hour and after the main dish in its various forms has been consumed, they bring out the sweetmeat, custards and strange little pies, which are best left undescribed.

I once tucked into a beautiful curried meat and rice supper with nine other people. We enjoyed the supper but later everyone got an attack of amoebic dysentery. I think eight of the people died and I had an out-of-body experience, but, strangely enough, I recovered. It was later found that the 'chef' was a carrier of amoebic dysentery and so he'd unknowingly murdered at least eight people. That is the danger of eating or drinking in the Far East. The safest thing is to drink a well-known brand of beer with a sealed top on the bottle. This is usually quite safe, as the germs don't like beer and the sealed top keeps them out.

But let not this little story dissuade you from enjoying a meal in the mysterious East. If you eat at a well-known restaurant, or you know the chef – you are perfectly safe. It's the others that give Eastern food a bad reputation. However, one may say that you can risk your life eating fish and chips in the West. Care is the byword.

With those final words, I wish you a good appetite and a delightful, restful sleep – without the sleep being in any way permanent. Bon appetite!

"Ted – thanks – you took me to India. I'd like to go there sometime, although I got really sick when I foolishly ate on the streets in Thailand. Those memories make me reluctant to visit third world countries. Speaking of food – I don't have any dessert but one of my students gave me a box of Rogers' Chocolates." I passed him the box of packaged sweets.

"Victoria Creams. I don't care which one I get – they're all good. Oh, strawberry. You do spoil me. I remember getting gifts when I was a teacher."

I nibbled on my own chocolate and then blurted out. "Ted, can I share something that has been bothering me?"

"If it's bad news, wait until I finish this." He winked. "No really, please tell me."

I drank more wine for courage. "Last week, I went to Hilda's eightieth birthday party. You're probably lucky you missed it." Hilda was in the Rotary club, and Ted and I had reconnected at her husband's funeral.

"Ah yes – can't abide small talk. I'd much rather paint. Did they have good food there?"

"I don't think I noticed. I wasn't there long. I got cornered by Rosemary, and out of the blue, she said, 'Okay you slept with Ted, right?' She insinuated that I had done that because I was a gold digger."

"A what?"

"You know what I mean, Ted. I felt contaminated. I didn't even speak – I just walked out the door."

"Janet, I vividly remember you crawling in bed with me when I was sick last year."

"You were freezing – and I had my clothes on. And it felt lovely for both of us to feel safe to do that. But you know that anything else is not in the cards for us. Frankly, my dear, I'm not attracted to you in that way. My girlfriend tells me I'm into lanky cowboy types. I just wish those types were as interesting to talk to as you are. I'd say you and I are kindred spirits."

"I wouldn't object if you took your clothes off. I've had a lot of nudes pose for me in my classrooms over the years. The human body is beautiful at any age. I enjoy seeing the various packaging of all types of people."

"Exactly. Sometimes I think we're all just little kids playing dress-up."

"But that woman is a twit. I wish you'd told her off."

"I had to get out of there. I had a sick feeling that everyone in the room was thinking the same thing. But I do like Hilda, which is why I went."

Ted had his hands folded across his belly and his feet up in the air on the footrest. He was the picture of contentment.

"Janet, people will always talk about you because you're not the least bit traditional, and you'd rather play the piano or create in some fashion, than waste your time. If you don't mind, love – I think I have one more poem to share before you take me back to Carlton House."

"Sure, fire away," I said, pulling the pad of paper towards me.

Victoria Cream

Tonight was special. I had a dinner of shrimp and vegetables coddled in curry and followed superbly by a Victoria cream. It was coated with dark chocolate – as dark as midnight but it tasted like the food of the gods. The whole thing was illustrated by a seductive jazz tune with a cornet speaking words of its own. The mood was one of romantic bliss, so personal and seductive that I sat entranced. Music of such a fine calibre and chocolate of such great taste blends in the mind and becomes almost like a drug. Each has its own quality and each transposes the mind into beautiful thoughts.

I came for a dinner and ended up being transported to another world far removed from gross reality. Power and greed distort life, while chocolate and music transform it into a wonderful fabric. What joy it is to feel so decadent. The world of Victoria creams, quiet jazz and red wine have created a transformation in my being. What was originally a supper invitation, has turned into a magical interval in my life.

I put the notebook down and relaxed across from him. "Thank you, Ted. You've made my worries disappear. Would you like some tea for the road?"

Teaching Pointers

I felt drained as I climbed out of my car in the parking lot of Carlton House. I had just finished teaching piano to eight children in the neighbourhood. Since I didn't have children of my own, due to complications and a need for a hysterectomy in my twenties, I was very grateful to have young people in my life who I could be playful with. But there were two or three that didn't put any time into practising and I felt like I was spoon-feeding them. Was it ego talking when I started thinking things like, 'I'm meant to do more than this'? Why didn't I just relax and let them fall behind? Was that ego too, feeling I needed my students to be the best they could be?

I buzzed the intercom and was greeted by the receptionist. "Oh, Ted will be so glad to see you. He's in fine form tonight."

"Hi, Sally. What was he doing tonight?"

"Oh, I could just hear everyone laughing as he sang with Tiny, and she got up and danced. She's in a musical at the Senior's Activity Centre, so he's been encouraging her to practise."

"Those women he sits with are so hip. I hope I'm like that when I'm in my eighties."

I wandered up the empty hall and took the stairs, instead of the elevator, to the top floor, hoping I could work out my earlier frustrations before I saw Ted.

I let myself into Ted's beautiful corner room, knowing he likely wouldn't hear the doorbell. Ted was on the phone, but his face lit up when he saw me. "Guess who just walked in? That's right. She's wearing a long red coat and looks beautiful but a little tired. Yes, Barry, I'll talk to you tomorrow night. Ta Ta."

Ted gave me his full attention as I plunked myself on the leather couch, tossing my coat over a stack of books and magazines.

"How's Barry?" I asked. Barry was a long-time friend of Ted's who looked after Ted and his affairs, including his store and sales of his works. Since he was a retired lawyer, he tended to be protective of Ted, which supported Ted's creative flights. Although Barry lived in Salmon Arm, he came to visit at least once a month and phoned Ted every night. He loved Ted as much as I did.

"Barry is really getting into cooking. I think I'll go visit him and Tricia, and their dogs in a couple of weeks." He used the remote in his chair to hoist himself into a more comfortable position and said, "Dear, you *are* looking a little peaked. Anything happen today? Are you just in from teaching?"

"Oh Ted, it's not a big deal but I'm wondering, what did you do with kids that didn't want to work? I really don't seem capable of being tough with them."

"You know it's amazing you asked me this tonight. I almost forgot about what happened today. I had a visit from a man I taught twenty-five years ago in the Yukon. Such a delightful chap. He walked into the store and said, 'Do you remember me?' and I said, sure I do – you're Darth Vader."

"Wow. You recognized him twenty-five years later?"

"We had coffee on the patio of Starbucks this afternoon. When he came into my class, he was about fifteen years old. He had been kicked out of most of his other classes and the school wanted to kick him out entirely because he was so disruptive. When he appeared that first day, he was dressed as Darth Vader. He was itching for a fight but I simply said 'Hi, Darth, you've come to the right place, because today we're painting landscapes, with a focus on the sky. You could always do the night sky, or whatever you like.' But he was having none of it. He just sat with a surly, bored look on his face. Everyone else was busily working at their easels so I went over and sat beside him. I chatted to him about Star Wars and how interesting it is to imagine other worlds beyond our tiny world. To make a long story short, I soon realized how extremely intelligent Rodney was. That was his real name and I just loved talking to him. I think he was just needing someone to believe in him. That's basically what Rodney told me today. That if it weren't for me, he'd probably have ended up on the street, or working in a factory or something, and instead, he is a very successful businessman in New York with a wife and two kids, and a very positive outlook on life."

"Oh Ted, you must have felt so proud and excited to see him again. I wish I could have met him."

"You can – we're having breakfast together tomorrow and I want you to join us. But what you want to realize as a teacher is that you're doing far more than teaching them to play the piano. You're giving them confidence, with your kind interest. And you're encouraging creativity, which not enough teachers do. I'm sure you must have people from your past come and tell you that."

"Occasionally, but I wish I could relax like you obviously were able to, when kids aren't behaving in a respectful way. I nearly lost it today."

"Well, maybe you should lose it. Some kids need that too."

I smiled at my sweet friend. "Ted, I can't stay long. I'm going to go home and make myself dinner and have a long bath. But I wanted to stop in since I was so close and see what you're up to. Sounds like you've had a great day. Do you want to write about it?"

"I wouldn't mind, but first, why don't you get a Guinness for us to split?"

I went over to the kitchen area and found two clean glasses, filling them with the creamy brown ale. "Good idea, Ted," I said, clinking my glass with his. "Guinness is a meal in itself."

Ted sipped from his glass and then set it down on the side table. With his hands folded over his sizable tummy, he began to speak as he stared out the window.

Scenes from My Window

In the morning, I awake, luckily, and I gaze over the street outside, bathed in the morning sunlight – or should I say, almost drowned in the morning sunlight. What has been a world of darkness is now bright with an early morning shine.

I sit in my dressing gown while others go to work in cars. The particular red car, which sits out all night, has disappeared. I don't know where the driver works but he's soon lost in the swirl of traffic going down Oak Bay Avenue. Then people appear walking on the sidewalk, heading for who knows where. How can they be about so early? I have only reached my twentieth yawn and they are walking briskly to some destination.

Buses trundle past with faces peering out of the windows, no doubt yawning, as it's too early to begin life. Suddenly, the air is rent with a call of sirens as an ambulance speeds down the road. Someone has had an early morning heart attack. I hope they live to see the evening. Then, outside my door, I can smell bacon and other delicious goodies being cooked in the kitchen downstairs. Oh, what a scent to come up from the corridors. The smell of bacon and sausages is as great as the scents of ancient Egypt, yet no one can buy the bottled scent of bacon and eggs. We can only imagine it. Some lively soul is playing music on the radio, which provides a wonderful backdrop to the morning scene. Blackbirds congregate on the telephone wires while gulls shriek and wheel past them and stand magnificently on top of the poles looking down at the other birds.

I bestir myself with a guilty feeling. As my age lengthens, my laziness increases. However, it is a delight to be lazy and retired. I only work when it pleases me and I also shirk when it pleases. With the mixture of shirk and work, I stumble through life quite happily, and soon, the morning gives way to afternoon when I paint and enjoy creating another world on canvas.

Gradually, after the creation of my world, I succumb to a beautiful idleness and lie back on the recliner to fall asleep.

Sometimes I dream and when I wake, the view from my window looks like another dream. It is now that my mind realizes how wonderful my life is. Everything is movement mixed with joy and sadness. And so, life continues with light and dark in equal measure until the sun, which has made the world visible, disappears below the horizon, and I sit and gaze at the moon, which has usurped its place in the heaven. There is the adventure of another day waiting in the wings. So, I fall asleep contented and happy.

"And now *I* feel contented and happy, thanks to you, Ted," I said as I shoved my notebook and pen into my oversized purse. "It could be the Guinness, but I suspect it's you."

Ted and I polished off our glasses and I said, "I really should go now."

"Well, just before you do, would you mind if we do one more since you've got me thinking about children?"

I reached for my notebook again. "Fire away, my dear!"

The Giggles of Children

I saw a group of children dancing on the green and singing a nursery rhyme. They sang and sang, and laughed and laughed, and their laughter rose in the air, and floated off and landed among a group of adults who were seriously shopping. The children's giggles entered the adult's bodies and they too began to giggle and laugh, and soon, the whole village was convulsed in mirth and everyone became happy and free without knowing why. Even the dogs barked with mirth and the cats mewed happily. The whole place was electrified with this feeling of joy.

What a magical morning. Even serious old men hobbling along with their walkers chuckled at the memories of youth. And old women with white hair smiled as they remembered former lovers and happy days spent in the meadow. Those little peals of laughter created a world of delight into the late afternoon, when everyone wended their way home and told merry tales over their supper before finally going to bed and dreaming of happy tomorrows.

"I love that, Ted. It reminds me of a movie I saw where the woman cooks with love and everyone that eats her food becomes more loving. Actually, it got quite sexy because some were overcome with amorous feelings."

"Well, of course, food is permeated with the vibrations of the chef. The same is true of all art. That's why people like what you and I do."

"Because we've got good vibes?"

"Staying positive is not always easy but keep thinking of what you're grateful for."

"I agree – it's the secret to life. I've got to get out of here, and I'm afraid I can't come for breakfast tomorrow. I've got a couple of students in the morning."

"Breakfast?"

"Rodney – remember?"

"I've got to get a great big calendar, and then remember to read my appointments. I'm getting rather forgetful."

"Here. I'll write you a note and put it on the floor so you can't miss it."

"I think he said he'd come by at 9:00. Thanks."

"Enjoy your time with him." I leaned over to kiss him.

"Pet, I'm so glad you came over. I'll call you tomorrow night."

The Fall

We were spinning down the highway to Sidney on a balmy day in May. I had suggested we go for a walk using his walker and Ted said he preferred to go out for lunch. So I chose Sidney, knowing they had beautiful cement walkways along the sea and we could always go to the Beacon Landing for lunch. Maybe, I could even inquire about getting another gig there.

"I'm glad you chose Sidney to go to. I haven't been to that town in ages."

"You probably won't recognize it then, Ted. And after they put in the new hotel, they put in a new band shell and green space along the water. It will be the perfect place for you to have a good walk. You've got to keep exercising. Are you still getting Bing to come, and massage you and manipulate your knee?"

"Oh yes, Bing. Wonderful man. And because of him, my knee was much better. But I kept forgetting I'd made an appointment with him. The poor man was very nice about it but after a couple of times, he stopped making the home visit. It's a shame. I really enjoyed talking to him about Chinese philosophies, and he knows what he's doing."

"If it weren't for him, I probably wouldn't still be playing the piano. He was an orthopaedic surgeon in China, so he knows his stuff. If you like, I'll take you to his office, although there are a few stairs up to the front door. You might have to go back to exercise class first."

"Isn't there a lot of traffic?" said Ted, staring out the windows and ignoring my suggestions about exercise. I was hoping I could talk him into walking more than a block before lunch. "What happened to the Waddling Dog? I love that name. And do you know I even took Maggie to visit that dog once."

"You sure loved your Maggie dog. What kind of dog was she?"

"A Paisley Terrier. She was the sweetest thing. I named her after Margaret Thatcher as she was a yappy little bitch."

I laughed. "You crack me up. Did you have a dog when Charles was growing up?"

"Yes, we did have a dog in Whitehorse. Brunhilda. She was the black dog who I would often paint in my earlier paintings. I used to walk Bruni in a park near our Porter Creek house. I called the forest Tulgey Wood which is where Alice in Wonderland chased after the rabbit. Charles didn't get as attached to dogs as I did. Or maybe he just didn't show it in the same way." We came to a stoplight and Ted waved to the kids sitting in the back seat of the vehicle in the next lane. They laughed and waved back.

I parked the car in a big parking lot by the sea and got Ted's walker out of the trunk. Soon, we were on a flower-lined path along the seawall, enjoying the magnificent view. Suddenly, Ted's pants fell down around his ankles. A couple walking past looked horrified but when we both started to laugh, they gave us a weak smile and hurried away. Once I got Ted's pants up, I held onto them and we careened to the restaurant. When we were seated, I was still laughing.

"I'm so glad you're having a good laugh at my expense," said Ted between giggles. Every time we looked at each other, we would chuckle. I kept patting away my tears with the cloth serviette.

"It was the look on that couple's face that got me the most," I said.

I had apologized to the two women sitting beside us a few minutes before but we were still out of control. One of them finally said, "You've got to tell us what's so funny. We need a good laugh."

Ted explained what happened, in his colourful way, and then they were laughing. We ended up pushing the two tables together and having a jolly time. We enjoyed some fish and chips, and even talked to the owner, who was curious about our noisy glee.

On our way back to the car, we stopped at a bench along the sea as Ted thought we should write about our experience. I pulled my journal from my purse.

The Fall

The sun was shining as I walked with my friend down the streets of Sidney. Then I began to boast about having lost weight. No sooner had the boast floated from my lips than my pants floated down to the ground. I was too late to save them.

Luckily, my underpants were extremely clean and blue in colour so they were acceptable to the eye by my companion. What a surprise! I had slimmed more than I guessed and without a belt, my slender form had shed the corduroy pants. Fortunately, the street was almost empty so only my companion noticed my predicament. She gave way to peals of laughter and I was forced to smile but suffered no embarrassment because they had fallen quite naturally as if preprogrammed for that very minute. I hastily gathered up the waistband of the pants, and found that by keeping my hand in the pocket and by my companion holding them at the back, they did not fall again.

So, I walked the rest of the way with her arm around my waist – not cuddling the form but holding up my pants. Luckily, they remained up for the rest of the afternoon and after a hearty meal in a good restaurant, my form filled up somewhat and served to curb any further embarrassment.

Pants may fall anytime and it could have been a disaster but really became a source of merriment and lightened the memory of the walk. I resolved that next time I go for an amble with my friend, I should wear a strong leather belt. However, the second walk will not be as interesting or as dramatic.

As we were returning home that afternoon, I said, "You make friends so easily, Ted. And you made sure everyone you met had a lovely experience. But you never did get your exercise. I bet you intentionally forgot that belt."

"Not exactly, but it's hard to make yourself do something when it hurts. I resist pain whenever I can."

"Oh, now you're trying to make me feel sorry for you," I teased. "You've got to stay strong, and as mobile as possible. My hiking group walks about ten kilometers in two hours and some of them are in their seventies. They say things like – 'exercise is the only option if you want to be independent.' You know, the 'use it or lose it' philosophy – and they're not talking about pants."

"Ha! I appreciate that you care, Jan," he said as I pulled the car through the gates of Carlton House. "Would you like to come up for a little visit?"

"I should really get going, Ted. I've got to practise for a gig tomorrow. But I'll see you up to your room. You can have a nap before dinner."

Once we were in his room, Ted eased himself down into his comfy chair.

"It's my uncle's eightieth birthday next week. Before I go, maybe you could say something about being in your eighties."

"Yes, and when you write to him, say hello from me. He'd be welcome to visit me if ever he's out this way."

I pulled my journal from my purse and laughed again when I saw the first line of 'The Fall'.

Octogenarians

We, who have lived through eight decades, see the world in simple terms. Not ruled by passions and uncontrolled thought. Our little barques have weathered great storms and now lie at anchor in calm harbours. Those who did not weather what the seas of life threw at them, lie wrecked on distant beaches in other times.

We once had shipmates who shared our trials and joys. But now the harbour is reached and there is only one at the helm. Age brings peace and calm content.

I watch the traffic speed by, heading for God-knows-where. I shall never drive again and that is another burden less in life. My transport is my scooter – bright red and glowing with happiness. I wave a banner and launch myself along the sidewalks to reach nearby destinations.

An octogenarian can handle the walking speed of a scooter. Greater ambition requires a taxi. But life is only as limited as your imagination. At night, I dream of distant lands and coloured adventures, more wonderful than daylight visions bring.

To be an octogenarian is not so bad. In the vicinity of Paradise, one functions as if one were already there.

I watched as Ted drifted off to sleep. He was the quietest sleeper I'd ever met. I knew that his Dreamworld was extra special so I quietly let myself out and returned to my life of practising piano and studying the meaning of life. Ted was the best teacher of the latter.

New Clothes and Strangers

We were driving up Yates Street discussing the men's clothing store we were heading for. Ted had said several times that he wanted me to take him to buy some classy clothes. Because he had such short arms and legs for his size, all shirts and pants would need alterations.

"Ted, maybe what you really need is classy but comfortable sportswear. After all, how often do you go out on the town?"

"Well, when I do, I want to look my best and I'm tired of what I have."

"You sound like a woman. Women spend much more than men on clothing and according to an article I read in Forbes Magazine, for most men, shopping for clothes is like doing your own brain surgery."

"Exactly – that's why you're coming with me."

"Maybe you've been here before – Philip Nyren. It has modern styles, and daring colours and textures. It's probably expensive too."

I pulled into the parking lot of the store, lifted Ted's walker out of the trunk, and was bringing it around to Ted's door when a salesman came running out. I had phoned ahead to make sure someone would be available to help us. Oh, no, I thought. Now we're in for it. This feels like we're in a used car lot.

The man opened Ted's door and said, "You must be Mr. Harrison – Welcome. I'm William, at your service." He was probably in his sixties, but he had dyed red hair, and was dressed in a lime green shirt and multi-coloured tie, and even had on lime green socks. I winked at Ted who was probably wondering if he'd forgotten it was St. Patrick's Day, but we had passed that a couple of months before. Ted stared at his socks before he reached for his walker to get out of the low seat.

Ted was seated on a couch in the main salesroom, and several inappropriate items of clothing were held in front of Ted by William and another, younger man. I could hear Ted saying, "No I don't think so," as I wandered around looking at the selection on the racks.

Finally, I sat beside Ted and said, "How about a nice tweed jacket, warm pants and a couple of colourful shirts."

"Yes," agreed Ted. "I like tweed – blue, with just a touch of purple."

William led Ted into a change room with the jacket, pants, a blue striped shirt and a pink one. I lost myself in a crossword puzzle until I heard William say, "Mr. Harrison, is everything alright?"

"Not really," was Ted's muffled reply.

I opened the change room and closed it with a wave to William. Inside, Ted was half dressed as he struggled to get his feet into the pants, unable to stand on one leg.

"Sit down, Ted," I said, realizing that he was used to having help when he got dressed. "I'm sorry – I should have been in here with you. Aren't these lovely pants?"

We got them up and both got the giggles when we looked at him in the mirror. The sleeves of the pink striped shirt hung to his knees and the pants were about a foot too long. "Are you sure this is what you want, Ted?"

Immediately, William said, outside the door, "The seamstress is here to pin your clothes to the right length, Mr. Harrison." We opened the door and William passed Ted the walker. Ted leaned on it patiently while the girl quickly put the pins in the required position. She did the same with the jacket.

"Very handsome," murmured the young woman as she gave one last pull to the sleeve of the jacket.

Ted studied himself in the mirror. "I love it. Let's go to the Faculty Club when these are finished, Jan."

"Sure, Ted. When should we pick them up?" I asked.

"We'll deliver them next Thursday to Carlton House," said William.

After we got Ted into his old clothes, he stood at the counter and struggled to pull out his wallet from his breast pocket. William came around and pulled it out for him, and even went through it to find the Visa. This man was making sure the sale happened.

When we got in the car, Ted sighed. "I have never spent so much on clothes in my life. The shirt alone was over one hundred dollars."

"Really? Ah, well, it's done now. And the material is soft. If it was a sheet, it would be a high thread count. All you have to do is enjoy them, and make sure you go out now and then. You should come to one of my gigs." We waited to merge into traffic. "Where to now?"

"Let's celebrate and go out for lunch. I need a change. You choose."

I drove along the Inner Harbour and Ted laughed when he saw Darth Vader playing the violin for the tourists. "I had a student that dressed like that."

"Oh yes, I wish I got to meet Rodney. See the Plaster Man?" I pointed to a figure frozen in position, covered in what looked to be white plaster. Even his face and hands had white goo on them.

"He looks like a statue," said Ted. "How long does he stand at one time? That takes discipline."

"He is actually a disciplined yogi. His mother brought him to our kundalini yoga class, and I was impressed with how agile and serene he was, for a guy. It takes years of meditation practise to get to that point and I believe, he must be meditating while he's doing what he's doing."

We stopped at a red light. "Would you look at that couple," said Ted. "They haven't come up for air yet." A young couple was kissing passionately, oblivious of their surroundings.

"Spring is in the air, Ted."

"I'll say. Where are we going?" he asked as he continued to watch the couple, craning his neck as we drove past them.

"I'm thinking Laurel Point might be fun since it's your day for spending. They have a fantastic outdoor patio with heaters and I can drive you right to the front door before I park."

A few minutes later, a young woman seated us beside a gas heater that looked like the Eiffel Tower. Although flags were flapping and the trees were waving to us, we were protected from the wind, and she had even given us blankets to put over our knees.

"I'm glad you thought of this," said Ted, gazing at the diverse action on the water. The big Blackball ferry to the United States was pulling out, two small harbour taxis were passing each other and a seaplane was coming in for a landing. People were walking along the pathway that wound around the Harbour.

The waiter came over. I knew him from the years I played there when they had a piano.

"Hey, Jan, great to see you again." I introduced Ted to Peter, who told us he was now the restaurant manager and this was his thirtieth year at the hotel. "I started here when I was in high school. I love the people industry."

"As I recall, you're very good at it," I said.

Ted glanced up from the menu. "We need a glass of white wine to celebrate this day. And are the crab cakes fresh?"

"You bet," said Peter. "How 'bout I bring you each a glass of Pinot Grigio on the house. We don't often have famous painters visit us."

"Most painters can't afford this place," laughed Ted. "I really appreciate that, young man."

We placed our order and were soon sipping wine and enjoying the holiday atmosphere.

As seemed to always happen when I was with Ted, the adventures continued. Two men were walking along the pathway, and one spotted me, waved and pointed me out to his friend. They both walked over to stand beside the railing of the patio.

"Ted, I met these two last night. They're just here for a few days from Fort McMurray and they're staying at the hotel

I was playing at last night. I'm sorry I don't remember your names but this is Ted Harrison."

"Wow, what an honour – I'm James," said the tall one wearing a Cowboy hat. "Mr. Harrison, you were my idol when I lived in the Yukon. I feel like I was supposed to meet you today."

"Maybe you were," I said. "We found ourselves coming here without planning it. Neither of us have been here in years."

"I'm Alex," said James's short, pudgy friend. His bulging eyes seemed to be absorbing every nuance.

Ted shook their hands but didn't suggest they join us.

"Well, we're going for a walk," said James, "but maybe we'll come and buy you dessert on our way back."

Ted was noncommittal as he waved good-bye. "How did you say you know them?" he asked.

"I don't really. I was playing in the restaurant at the Grand Pacific last night, and a woman was rather annoying, making schmaltzy requests and talking about her son and grandson to me while I tried to concentrate on what I was doing. While she was eating, and talking, she started choking. I stopped playing and said 'gosh, do you want me to hit you?'

"James and Alex heard that and started laughing and couldn't seem to stop. I'm not sure why. But at the end of the night, they gave me a hundred-dollar tip, which rarely happens to me. I chatted to them on my break and they bought my C.D. They told me they make a lot of money in Fort McMurray and come here twice a year to spend some of it."

"I seem to recall you like cowboy types. Are you attracted to James?"

I grinned. "He is rather sweet eh? But no more long-distance relationships for me. Besides, he's probably married."

Our meals arrived and Peter put them in the middle of the table so that we could share.

Ted looked at the tuna salad and said, "That is so beautiful, even if it tastes terrible it will be worth the price. Let's start with the crab cakes."

We savoured every mouthful. Ted said, "I can't tell you how wonderful it is to enjoy all these flavours and textures."

"I thought you liked the food at Carlton House."

"Oh, it's great but they do have to cater to people with sensitive stomachs, and the menus repeat themselves which is natural in a large residence."

We sipped and ate in companionable silence. After a time, Peter removed our empty plates and we sat with our wine.

"I hope you brought your writing book with you," said Ted.

"Sure, are you going to speak about the Heimlich manoeuvre?"

"I presume she didn't need that?"

"No, it all worked out, of course."

Love on the Street

I thought they were statues constructed by an imaginative artist seeking the spirit of love as his muse. I cannot say the kisses were passionate because I saw only one kiss and it lasted well over a minute, so I presume they were in love. Then we passed them in the car, and they were still standing statuesque and romantic on a drab street. They were so still that if a dog had passed, he would have mistaken them for a fire hydrant. However, nothing untoward happened and we continued on our way.

I didn't know how they breathed. I myself am only allowed three-second kisses because any longer would lead me into temptation and other interesting paths. However, they have proven food for thought and in the middle of the night when the moon shines down, I shall see them still standing in the same spot, statuesque and immobile. Love without action and probably action without love.

"I need to visit the boy's room," said Ted.

"Can you make it on your own?" I asked, bringing his walker to him. "It's a bit of a walk up the hall and to the right."

"I'll figure it out," said Ted. He leaned into his walker and I watched him move from one side of the hall to the other.

Rereading what Ted had dictated, I thought about how playful Ted's musings were. I looked around at other diners on the patio, speculating on whether they were tourists or lovers or business acquaintances. Ted would have a story for each of them.

Just then, James and Alex reappeared. I invited them to sit with us but before they sat down, I said, "James, would you mind going to the men's washroom to make sure Ted is okay? I really can't go in there and he's been a while."

Alex and I shared some small talk but I was worried. Finally, I stood up and walked down the hall. There was Ted conversing and laughing with James who had his arm around Ted as he guided the walker in a straight line.

James insisted on buying us coffee and dessert. We spent another half hour on the patio, hearing about their Fort McMurray life, which sounded like a strong community, and of course, James shared his story about being a kid when he met Ted for the first time at his public school.

"Ted, I don't know if you realize what an impression you made on us kids. You were such a cool guy we couldn't help but respect you. You encouraged us to express ourselves without fear."

Alex said, "I'm sorry, folks, but we have to go. We booked a whale-watching tour." James looked disappointed but he stood up with Alex. They each gave me a hug and shook Ted's hand.

"Such a pleasure to meet you, Sir," said James. They gave us one final wave from the seaside pathway after leaving the building.

Peter came over to tell us our lunch had been paid for by the gentlemen.

"Wow, aren't we lucky?" I said. "I hope they come to my gig tonight. Maybe I'll get another tip."

Ted accepted a second cup of coffee and suggested one more poem.

Strangers

I love going to coffee shops and tiny restaurants where one can meet strangers. We know our friends but strangers are not yet friends because we do not know them and yet one can become fairly intimate with them and their thoughts.

First of all, one must overcome shyness and not be tongue-tied. See them as fellow human beings. We're all on the same path of life and often we require new experiences.

There are things that often help when communicating with strangers. For example, think of a dog, a cat or even a canary. One can reach a stranger through his or her pets. And people enjoy talking about their pets because they're the closest animal beings they know. Your dog or cat sees you popping into the bath – they see you without your clothes. They see you going to bed and rising the next morning. They see all the intimate details of your life. So, to make friends with the animal is to make friends with the person. And people often have the same characteristics as their pets. I have met people who should be swimming in an aquarium. Their mouths open and close without much information coming through while people with yackety dogs often talk endlessly about nothing in particular.

A stranger, once the key to their personality is found, can shed new light on an aspect of life, which has not been considered closely. The quiet gentleman sitting on a seat may actually be a Buddhist priest meditating upon the infinite. I have met spiritual people sitting quietly in the corner of a coffee shop. They leisurely stir the coffee but their minds are pitched on an infinite plain. The quality of a fine mind can only be guessed at by the look in their eyes and the accompanying body language. The stranger is not always a strange being or removed from you by sitting in another sphere of thought. In fact, on talking to them, you often end up feeling related in many aspects of life. They suddenly say, "Oh, I feel that too! I too have seen the Pyramids and gazed into the eye of the Sphinx." And so, a bond is created. "Oh, is that where you come from. I had an auntie who went to the same school. I had an uncle who was also in the Navy. I had a friend who got drunk in the same pub …" And instantly, they cease to be strangers and become friends. You end up patting the dog, tickling the cat and kissing the goldfish. Behold, the stranger has been turned into a friend and you both feel all the better for the experience.

I closed the notebook and drank the last of my coffee. "Ted, I'm going to bring the car around now. We've had a long day."

"I've loved every minute of it. Well, perhaps, I could have done without that change room but now that it's over, I can laugh about it. What did you think of that chap's lime-green socks?"

"Rather flamboyant, but at least we're not going to forget him in a hurry. I bet you were tempted to get purple socks."

I brought the walker over to Ted and said, "Here you go. Take your time and I'll be waiting out front for you."

As I sauntered to the parkade, I had a smile on my face, picturing Ted in that dressing room with the clothes swirling down his short arms and legs.

Valentine's Day

"Happy Valentine's Day, Ted," I said, tossing my coat on the couch as I leaned in to kiss him.

"How nice to see you, love – you look gorgeous. Have you been out with a man? Oh, turn that TV off please."

"Are you sure you're not in the middle of something?"

"Much rather talk to you, although if you'd come an hour ago, I might have had to finish my program. Is that a new dress?"

I smiled. "I only wear dresses if I have a gig, it seems."

"Where was it?"

"It was just a short cocktail party at Government House. I got to play with my lovely friend, Joey. He usually plays bass but he played guitar this time. Remember, you met him when we went to the pub. He plays in lots of bands."

"The southern gentleman. Where was he from?"

"Chattanooga, Tennessee – don't you love that name? I always thought I'd like to be from Kuala Lumpur. It sounded so exotic – but when I got there, I found it wasn't all that romantic."

"Malaysia is dirty and behind the times but I did enjoy myself there."

"We're both pretty good at finding the juice in a situation. I brought you a Valentine," I said, handing him a card and a chocolate heart.

"Thank you. I didn't get you anything but you know how I don't shop."

Ted opened the card and smiled at the sentiment. He immediately opened the chocolate and had a large bite.

"I know you're not supposed to eat sugar but a little bit should be okay. You could always save half for tomorrow."

"Are you kidding? It's delicious. Thank you." After licking his lips, he said, "What was going on at Government House?"

"It was the Book Awards. We just played before they had a sit-down dinner. I love doing that. And we had a trumpet player join us who was masterful. Miguelito – he's from Cuba, and plays with such sensitivity and passion."

"Don't you have an interesting life? Although, I am surprised to see you here on a night like tonight. You should be out with a wonderful man."

"I am," I said, "but I'm not staying long. What happened to you today? Were you at the store?"

"I was. I took the scooter down. Oh, yes, and I plowed into a sign and knocked it over on the Avenue. But the lady who owned the restaurant it was advertising was very nice about it."

"I'm glad you're not trying to drive your car anymore."

"I nearly forgot to tell you. I sold the car today. I'll just take cabs when I need to."

"Congratulations, Ted. You're handling it well. Do you feel a little sad about it?"

"Not in the least. It's been sitting in the garage for months. I had become a terrible driver. Now I can relax."

"Do you want to write about anything before I head home for some dinner?"

"Why don't we go down the street to the pub?"

"It will be crowded since it's Valentine's Day."

"That's right. Well, I'll speak about today then."

"Fire away, Ted," I said, finding a scrap of paper and a pencil.

Saint Valentine

Today, I ate a chocolate heart given by my Valentine. Of all the things that stand for love, a heart is still the best. Whether it is of chocolate, paper, plastic or any material, the symbol means love and that one heart equals a lot of love.

I don't know what St. Valentine did but I think he was tame compared to the Greek goddess of love. I mean, she really did the rounds. She was in everybody's bed – or whatever they slept on in ancient Greek times. St. Valentine is the Christian symbol for love, but maybe he did nothing because physical love is decried in the Bible, so maybe he represents asexual love. They wouldn't have nuns in the world if they were going to have sexual love.

Take, for example, a nun's habit. It's the most asexual dress you can think of with the black for no action and the white for purity. It doesn't awaken the senses, except at a funeral. It stops the nuns from getting into bad habits.

To the ancient Greeks, love was free and joyful – and they certainly didn't wear a uniform. The toga was the normal dress but when they had sex, they took it off.

Despite the restraints and teachings about sin, sex still goes on and people just carry on as their ancestors did. Otherwise, we wouldn't renew the race. If sex is so wicked, why are there so many people in the world?

We spend a lot of time running around in motorcars and often the back seat is used as a love bed. It's not a perfect place to make love though, since one has to keep ones' mind on the road.

'The King of Love, my shepherd is.' This doesn't mean physical love. It means love that embraces humankind. But real love is where humanity embraces physical love. Little pigs make love – and it's purely sexual love – designed to increase the number of piglets. But since man has moral issues about sex, love feelings must be sincere so that we're not doing it for the fun of it. When you cut the fun out of sex, it becomes quite serious.

The first thing the hippies did was to stop worrying about moral issues. They certainly enjoyed themselves, but they found they were getting diseases they'd never thought about, so the diseases made them question if it was worthwhile having coitus for the fun of it. This is an example of human beings, by their own actions, being brought back to having lives of restraint or discipline.

If we go too far in describing physical love, it becomes immoral, and then the censors come and limit what we should do, and give us all a guilty conscience. Freest sex is in the mind – not the body. But we need to be disciplined or the whole world would be on a romp.

Tonight, I took a prostate pill and ate a chocolate heart. This should lead to the grossest immorality and yet I feel quite calm. I'll recommend them to St. Valentine.

It's lucky that we have a Valentine's Day because it causes young people to suggest love as an important subject in their lives – so Valentine gives us that excuse. There are many shades of meaning to the name of St. Valentine. I'm afraid I know too little about his life to wade through the mass of morality, which it engenders. However, everyone is free to explore the matter on their own which should lead to benign thoughts.

Valentine is for any taste. You can moralize about it or take the view that it means absolute freedom and that is where we have a problem that is constantly coming up in our society. Shall I or shall I not?

Ted opened his eyes and said, "Hey, I just remembered that Ken was here yesterday and brought me some food from his restaurant. Why don't you load up a plate and put it in the microwave? I'll never eat it."

"Now you're talking, Ted. I love Ken's food." I opened up various Chinese Food containers and put some of each into a bowl. "How about you?"

"Sure – just a little bit would be fun, although dinner was beautiful tonight."

"You're so lucky that you have the chef from the Swiss restaurant here. When I was married, we walked up there after teaching every Thursday night. It was just a block away."

"I know I'm lucky and I'd be luckier if you could find me a Guinness to share with you."

"Well, what do you know?" I said, as I split the large can.

I greedily ate from my bowl while Ted picked at his. I knew he was just keeping me company.

"Thank you for dinner – it's delicious. Did you get some painting in today, Ted?" I asked.

"I started to when I was in the store, but then the most interesting family came in and we had a long talk and a cup of tea, and then I needed to come back here for a snooze."

"That must happen a lot. But you don't seem to like painting here as much, do you?"

"I can't seem to get into it here. Maybe just because I miss my studio at home." He put his bowl aside and shakily lifted the Guinness to his lips. Still holding the glass, he relaxed back and smiled. "I'm so glad you're here. You know, before you arrived, I was watching a TV show that was so interesting that it keeps coming back to me in my mind. I believe that's rather rare."

"I wouldn't know. I don't have a television and I don't miss it. I can always come over here and watch it with you."

"That's true, although there's too much to talk about. May I speak about this?"

"Of course, Ted. There's no more food, so let's write."

Television

Television is abhorrent to many people who pride themselves on their intellectual storehouse of learning and sensibility. However, the other night, I gazed on a scene of such magical reality that had only existed in my imagination before. This was a journey to the edge of the universe. The spectator was lifted up from the earth, and shot into outer space with amazing speed and wondrous vision. The moon and its craggy rocks were soon by-passed and on we went to the planets in the solar system. Venus – which sparkles jewel-like in the sky appeared as a full ball of gas, its surface surging with raging storms and winds far mightier than those on Earth.

Then, onwards we went to visit Saturn and its moons. Huge blocks of ice in the rings crashed together and formed tiny ice boulders, which added to the number ringing the planet. What a frightening world it appeared to be. All the sounds of wind and movement taking place thousands of light years from Earth. We passed through the mighty forces and flames of our sun, and then ever onwards to the edge of our planetary system.

We now entered a really mysterious area where the remains of long dead planets circled and Earth had become a lost world we could not see. The huge forces of distant planets were at work, causing us to be a bobbing cork in a wild ocean. Finally, we reached a thousand light years from Earth and went on to even greater distances in time. After a journey of thousands upon thousands of light years, we arrived at a mysterious area of flaming stars and whirling celestial bodies. We had gone back in time thousands of years – nay – millions! Since before the dinosaurs and even before Earth was created.

At last, we witnessed a white star, one spoonful of whose mass would weigh thousands of tons. This was the big bang. The white star suddenly exploded with a mighty roar and the mass disintegrated at thousands of miles an hour. Even today, it is still expanding, although it began millions of years ago. When it finally stops, our world may be long gone as our sun will have died and become a white dwarf. No one will know we ever existed. Even God won't be there!

"I wish I'd seen that show with you. It sounds amazing. I love looking at the stars and imagining other life forms up there. I'm sure we can't be the only ones in this huge universe. What would you do if an alien invited you into his space ship?"

"Well, I'd go, of course. I'm sure they'd be much more sophisticated than we are. And I doubt if they have the ridiculous wars and animosity that we have."

"I read somewhere that the basis of all wars is jealousy. There's a community in Portugal that is working on that by allowing free love amidst the families living there. I'm afraid I can't get my head around that but I do believe jealousy is worth working to eliminate," I said.

"Perhaps, it would be paradise then, and it would be rather boring?" suggested Ted. "I know you have to go – you've had a long day – but I'd like to have you write one more little thing, if you don't mind."

"Of course."

My Paradise

My paradise lies on Oak Bay Avenue. It is a room isolated from reality. The outside world can only be reached by looking through a window, which is usually shuttered.

I lie and look on the ceiling, which contains one thousand images. As if in a hypnotic trance, I finally awake. The doorbell rings and my dreams are displaced for a moment until the earthly matters are dealt with.

All this is true save when Jan arrives. She brings with her a world of dreams, which is in stark contrast to the more mundane presence of others who call. Without hearing a sound, she brings music to my life.

Although the day is dull, her smile radiates around the room, lighting up the darkest corner. And my heart responds with joy and a strange delight.

"Ted, that was the nicest Valentine you could have given me. Thank you so much."

Ted simply sat, like Buddha, with a benevolent smile.

"I'm going to head off now. Your girls will be here soon to make sure you've taken your medicine."

"Thank you again, my Angel. Do come back soon. Perhaps, we should plan a little excursion somewhere."

"Good idea, Ted. Phone me and we'll look at our calendars." I kissed him and walked down the hall, no longer sad that I didn't have a date on Valentine's Day. My life was rich.

Contentment

Ted shuffled through my kitchen into the living room. "It smells so good in here. What's cooking?"

"I decided to roast a chicken. Then I can have some leftovers this week. I don't cook like this for myself."

"I don't blame you. I'm so grateful someone else is worrying about that at Carlton House." He plopped into the old blue chair, looking around. "Super Dupe – you've got the fireplace going. You need a dog curled up in front of it. Why don't you have a dog, Jan?"

I sat across from him after fiddling with the computer to get some jazz ballads playing. "The landlord doesn't allow pets. I'm not sure I would have one even if I could though. I'd have to figure out dog sitters when I go away. And it's expensive, isn't it? Though, probably not as expensive as having a boa."

"You mean a snake?"

"Didn't I tell you about Cuddles? I was in a travelling show band for a year and since we did an Alice Cooper set, we had a boa constrictor. He was the only nice guy in the band. I had to buy him rabbits and rats for his meals because no one else bothered with him. The cleaning ladies at the hotels we stayed at would run out screaming when they saw who I was sharing a room with."

"You should write a book about all your experiences as a musician," Ted said, once he stopped laughing. "Maybe you need to get a dog to see what it's like to have a warm-blooded pet. I'm thinking of getting one. Then you can enjoy mine. I'll have to move to the main floor if one of the apartments becomes available."

"Would you manage to lean over to pick up his poop?" I asked.

"That's a good point. Here comes a poem. I'm going to try to make it rhyme."

I grabbed a pen.

An Ode to Manure

When you're bending, you have to stoop,
But not when picking up elephant poop.
An elephant can drop a load,
On path or meadow, street or road,
And then you put it in a sack
And trundle it to where the greens are growing thinner,
And look towards their gourmet dinner.
While all your vegetables just sit,
Waiting for their gourmet shit.
Alas, this is a filthy rhyme,
To wade into this verbal slime.
My garden loves this calm caress
And thrives upon the putrid mess.

"How cool, Ted. You can rhyme without trying. Rather revolting, but fun."

"I'm sure I could do better if I tried a little harder."

"I think this type of spontaneous eruption that you do is a perfect way of showing how the creative process works and how you just never know when it will hit."

"Have you been writing music lately?"

"Not much, but the other night, I was walking around Queenswood at dusk and an owl started to hoot, and I started singing that rhythm and interval, and then a little melody came. When I got home, I used that in my improvisation."

"Did you call it 'Who Cooks for You?'"

I laughed. "I know bird-watchers call it that. Actually, I realized after I played it doesn't really resemble the call but it motivated me with the unusual chord that relates to their sound. It's a Major seventh with a sharped fifth and sharped eleventh, in case you're interested. Apparently, when owls are looking for a mate, they have a different call."

"Play it for me."

"It's different every time but I'd love your opinion. Thanks." I turned off the music and sat down at the piano. First, I played on the descending scale they often use, as an introduction, and then I played the minor, haunting melody. The chord progression was fun to improvise over so I went through it a couple more times. As I came towards the end, I thought about how easy it was to play for Ted. I never felt judgement, only support and interest.

"That was beautiful, love. Are you going to put words to it?"

"I'm not sure. Perhaps, you'd like to try putting some words to it?"

"Actually, it was more like a classical piece for me. I found different memories arose as you shifted the chords. I don't think you want words to that one. It reminded me of a Debussy piece. Do you happen to know *La Fille aux Cheveux de Lin*?"

"Nice accent, Ted. Girl with the Flaxen Hair. Sure, I'll see if it still sits under my fingers," I said, pulling out a classical book. "Debussy and Chopin were my favourites when I was at Western."

I was a little rusty but Ted leaned back with his eyes closed, his hands folded over his belly and a smile on his lips. When I was finished, he sighed. "What a treat to feel those vibrations rumbling through me. I love sitting right beside the piano while you play."

The wind was howling outside so I went over to the woodstove and threw on a couple more logs.

"I'm going to get your dinner, Ted. Would you like dark meat or light or both?"

"May I have a drumstick?"

"Sure, I'll have the other one. We'll pretend we're cavemen."

I turned on some ballads by Miles Davis. "I hope you like listening to trumpet."

In the kitchen, I took my time making gravy with the drippings and slicing the chicken. I was thinking how relaxed I felt preparing food for Ted, in contrast to the anxiety I would often have when I was with a partner. Was it just because I knew he didn't have any expectations and was grateful for any effort? Relationships could be so complicated.

I brought a tray into the dining room with the wine and gravy, and started to giggle when I found Ted already sitting at the table with his napkin tucked in. "You must be hungry," I said as I poured him some wine.

When I came in again and set his plate in front of him, he said, "How colourful. Beets, sweet potatoes, carrots and what are these?"

"Parsnips, to keep you sweet." I lifted my glass. "A toast to you, Ted."

"To me – why me?"

"Because you're so easy to hang out with."

I picked up my drumstick and chewed greedily. "What is it about bones that make you feel you can be as sloppy as you like?" I asked with a full mouth.

Ted wiped his fingers on his napkin and said, "I think it dates back to early man when tribes would unite around a beast they had killed. It was a celebration and as it cooked over a fire, they would dance and sing, and of course, they would eat the cooked meat with their hands. For us, something ancestral kicks in."

"Or maybe we have a flash of a previous life," I said.

"It's entirely possible," agreed Ted, pouring gravy over his veggies.

Miles continued to play his moody trumpet in the background as Ted methodically cleaned up his plate. I paid attention to the piano player's accompaniment. Red Garland could really swing when he pushed beats one and three, locking in with the bass and drums.

"Hey, Ted, I'm having a party next weekend. Would you like to come? It's on Saturday."

"It depends. Are you going to try to set me up again?"

"No, not this time. But what about all the lovely women at Carlton House? You could bring one. How about Tiny?"

Ted winked. "Yes, there are a couple of women I like there. But we all prefer staying friends. How many people are coming to your party?"

"I only have eight chairs, counting the piano stool, so there won't be more than that. So far, I've only invited four."

"Are they all musicians?"

"No, but one is an artist who teaches at a private school. He's actually really good – you guys might hit it off. And the food will be unusual – I love cooking for a gang. It drove my husband crazy that I like to experiment on guests. But heck, even a flop can be fun. Something to laugh about."

"Yes, I'd like to come," said Ted.

"Oh good. I'll get someone to pick you up."

"And will you give a concert after dinner?"

"If I invite musicians, we'll have a bit of a jam, no doubt," I said, taking our plates into the kitchen. When I returned, Ted was making his way to the blue chair.

I set his glass beside him and curled up on the couch. "Do you want to hear a classical recording Ted?"

"I'd like to hear you again."

I laughed.

"What's so funny?"

"I think you're the first man in my life who has asked me to play for him."

"That's ridiculous. Why did you choose men like that?"

I shrugged. "Feel like writing about something?" I asked, trying to change the subject.

"I *am* curious though, Jan. Because commitment usually includes interest in the other person's passions."

"I would agree with you, Ted. My first husband did admit years later that he was jealous of my passion for music, which is why he wouldn't even let me have a piano. Even though I was given a beautiful one by our neighbour when she moved. I ended up renting a separate little studio apartment so I could keep playing. And my second husband was very wrapped up in his own martial arts passion which I was fascinated by and enjoyed learning about."

"I think you just picked the wrong men."

I thought about that. "You know, I did have a short relationship with a much older, wonderful man who was an artist and he encouraged me to play, and he introduced me to some amazing jazz music."

"What happened to him?"

"He kinda dumped me when I started selling real estate. He said I was prostituting myself. He was probably right. I was so stressed for the couple of years that I did that. I didn't touch the piano, and had to let my students go."

Ted pushed the chair backwards so that his feet were as high as his head. "I'm ready to speak about something," said Ted.

I had barely found a pen before Ted began his slow, relaxed speech.

Commitment

Everything of value that one does is usually driven by a sense of commitment. If we play the piano well, it's due to a strong commitment to practise every day and gradually perfection or near perfection is achieved. However, it takes a strong commitment to do this over the years and then, if we take a leap into marriage, we promise to commit ourselves to the partner until 'death do you part'. But this commitment can fail through familiarity. We can often marry a different person to whom we thought we were marrying but this knowledge only comes with the familiarity gained through consorting with the other individual.

When we have a hobby, we can become so committed to it, that the hobby becomes a lifestyle and can actually change our lives whereas it was only a part-time thing at first. However, a commitment like marriage is totally different because you have chosen a different lifestyle to begin with. When you give a solemn promise to do something, that is a commitment, which can lead into different byways of behavior. If we have babies, the babies become a commitment and they grow into children who require a greater commitment. We are entrusted further when these children become teenagers. One may have trouble with spouses but it can fade in comparison with the trouble one can have with a teen.

So, we must beware of commitment and how binding it is, if we feel we don't have the strength to go through with it. There's many a blushing, glistening-eyed young lady who enters a commitment before thinking it out. Uncommitted virgins end up as plump housewives complaining of overwork and too little love because their committed choice of life has led them to become fat and overworked. Thus, romance is destroyed because of a feeling of commitment gone askew. However, deep friendships can grow and improve with time, and so, this commitment can bear fruit of a life-long friendship, which never changes but only grows more satisfying and blesses both of the committed partners. We need not be committed only to humans but also our pets. Who can resist a pleasant dog or cat that also becomes committed to us? Cats especially grow to respect one owner and can be quite belligerent towards others they do not know.

We all become committed to a lifestyle which is unique to us personally. A lion tamer is out of place looking after a canary. However, we can all become committed to our occupations. The artist is committed to his easel and paints, the musician to his instrument, and both commitments bring great satisfaction. We can, however, be so committed to what we believe in, that we become bores and bigots. That is why it is dangerous to try to seduce a person from their profound belief in order to follow your belief.

So, the lesson we can learn is, to be loyal to our commitment but to not attempt to change anyone else's commitment, which is personal.

I looked up from my messy scribble to see that Ted still had his eyes closed. I wanted to ask him about a couple of sentences I wasn't sure I caught but from past experience, I knew he wouldn't be able to go backwards. As I was rereading the last two paragraphs, Ted opened his eyes and said, "I've been enjoying Miles Davis but probably not in the same way that you might."

"What do you mean, Ted?"

"It's got me thinking about my days in the army."

"Did you listen to jazz in those days?"

"No, I'm thinking about the bugle. Do you mind if we try another poem?"

"Fire away, Ted."

The Trumpet

Of all the musical instruments, the trumpet is one of the most noble. It can be awfully sad or very bright. For instance, the army uses a trumpet extremely well – mainly the bugle. You wake up in the morning to Reveille, which is bright and cheerful but sounds awful when it's waking you up with its 'rise and shine get out of bed' sound. To be awakened harshly by a bugle is not the finest feeling in life. You can't even meditate after waking and there's nothing else to do but get out of bed and face the day with blind courage.

I had a friend much bigger than me and we used to have a race to the washroom. One special morning, he was ahead of me, and once he got past me, he turned around to laugh at me and didn't see a concrete pillar. He fell and collapsed, and I jumped over him and got to the washbasin first. He learned to never turn around while running. After that, we were fully awake.

In the evening, to summon 'lights out', the bugle would sound the Last Post before we slept. This is repeated every November 11th to honour all the soldiers that died in service. It has great meaning and awakens memories of comrades who have died and passed beyond.

So, the bugle is a very emotional instrument. It conjures moods – especially to a person who has seen military service.

The trumpet can play the most haunting classical music and the most vigorous jazz, and it's also great for special occasions like announcing the Queen. It has been used for centuries for greeting royalty and homecoming troops from Roman times to the present day.

The horn, I prefer above all others, is the French horn. It has a haunting melody, which gives a feeling of nostalgia to the listener. When we die and go to heaven, the trumpets sound for us on the other side. They don't play drums – it's always trumpets. They can denote a victory. When we finish our life, we've scored something – we've gotten through life without cracking.

The trumpets sound for us on the other side as we go through the myth of the Pearly Gates. If heaven is paved with gold, the sound of the trumpet is a symbol of the wealth and joy in the feeling one has after reaching Paradise. It's good to have a myth of this nature because death is the final experience of life. So, the myth may as well be a good one.

I set the journal aside and had another sip of wine. Ted opened his eyes and stretched.

"Ted, chances are you're going to die before I do. Do you think we could somehow have a meeting spot afterwards so I can ask you what it's all about? I've always been so curious about the ending of this relatively short life we have."

"If I possibly can, I'll connect with you. I promise."

"Is there anything on your bucket list that you still haven't done?"

"I have no regrets, if that's what you mean. But there are lots of places I'd like to see still. Or visit again."

"Would you like to go to England again?"

"Not really, now that my sister is gone. I'm happy for her that she has moved on. She was devastated when she lost her husband. That was a beautiful relationship, as far as I could tell."

"I love seeing people that are still in love years later. I play at a lot of anniversary parties, and you can recognize the ones that still respect and adore each other. They're usually very generous people."

"That's an interesting observation. Yes, I think one does have to be generous to stay happy about all the compromises that are necessary."

I switched the music channel and Barbra Streisand was singing *Smile* with Tony Bennett. "Ah, I love Tony," I said.

"I love Barbra," said Ted. "She sings effortlessly. Tony is working hard on that one."

We sat listening, and I felt a sleepy heaviness come over me as the fire crackled. Ted interrupted my dreams when he said, "I have one more thing for you to write before you take me back in this wicked weather."

"Sure, Ted," I said. "Good thing you woke me up."

Contentment

The warmth of a visit relieves the chilly winter night. Good wine, good food and music filling in the gaps. This is an evening of peace and unworldly bliss, which transcends the normal routine. Worry is cast aside and replaced by a quiet joy.

I see a picture in my mind while gazing at a masterpiece. Jan transcends the images of Mona Lisa because she is a living blessing whose smile has magic powers. These powers dissipate my worries and stress. Her smile showers me with blessings, which are soundless and magic in their elements. I am, indeed, fortunate to share a moment of contentment.

"Gosh, Ted, I'm going to get a fat head if you keep this up. Are you ready to put on your hat and coat and face the elements?"

The Dinner Party

I stirred the fresh basil into the bow-tie pasta salad and squeezed it into the fridge beside the stuffed salmon that just needed to be put in the oven for a half hour or so. I had been working on this party for two days: cleaning, reading recipes, buying food and wine, making two salads and a chocolate torte. I realized my breathing was shallow as I worried about what I'd forgotten. Well, at least I seemed to be prepared ahead of time so that I could relax and enjoy my guests. I now had an hour to myself and I intended to put on some fancy clothes.

The back doorbell rang and I looked at my watch. Now what? I opened the door to the carport and there was Ted, leaning on his cane. A taxi was pulling out of the driveway.

"Hello, Ted, I thought you were coming with Holly and Mark." I had called Holly and asked if they could swing by to pick him up, even though they had never met him. It was on their way and I knew they would be happy to.

"They did call but I wanted a chance to visit you."

"Great idea. Perfect timing. I could do with a drink and some down time."

Normally, I would be rattled by an early guest but I could feel myself relaxing. Ted felt like family. And not a dysfunctional one. Following him into the living room, I handed him his Guinness, clinked my wine spritzer against his glass, and had a refreshing drink before setting it down and flopping on the couch across from him.

Ted was still holding his glass and gazing at the creamy contents when I said, "It's going to be a fabulous party. I've been slaving more than usual but I know it will be worth it."

Ted put his glass down on the side table and said, "Why is this party so important to you?"

I paused and smiled at Ted's rather surprising question. I pondered whether to tell him the truth and finally said, "I've invited the two couples my husband and I used to like hanging out with. They haven't had much to do with me since Ray and I separated, and I know the men didn't approve of the way it all happened. They blamed me because I had an affair and broke my marriage vows."

"I believe affairs only happen when the marriage is not meeting the couple's needs."

"Maybe so, but it was a betrayal and I still feel terrible about it. And rather heartbroken. I think our marriage could have been amazing if he had been willing to communicate. By the last few years, we were living such separate lives, I knew I was foolish to hang in there and keep hoping. But I'd already flunked one marriage. I couldn't imagine going through another."

Ted was watching me carefully with his steady blue eyes. "What is your relationship like with your father?"

I laughed. "Gosh, Ted – are you going to analyze my psyche?"

Ted smiled and answered slowly, "Does your father respect you and support your endeavours?"

I stared out the window, barely noticing a couple walking by with two kids running and laughing in front of them. I had done enough therapy over the years to know I was neglected by my father and wasted a lot of energy trying to get his approval. Although I was sure I was ready for a normal, supportive relationship, maybe I still had more to learn. I said, "My Dad was probably pretty traditional for that time and he saw my choices as acts of rebellion."

"I suspect you keep trying to please the men in your life, possibly you're doing the same thing with the men you've invited, hoping to get them to approve of you again. I want you to be sure you're not trying to ally with people that don't respect you. You wouldn't be the first woman to have done so. But, darling – you are an exceptional person and you deserve to be supported by your friends. Please honour your own feelings rather than trying to please men at all costs to yourself."

"I appreciate what you're saying, Ted, and I *am* nervous about seeing my friends' husbands again tonight. I'm also wondering if I'm just trying to prove to everyone, including myself, that I have moved on and I'm happy. I've invited another couple – Joey and Di – and I *know* Joey respects and loves me. We've done gigs together for years. I think he's the best musician in town. I never would have thought to invite him because he's always working on weekends but I ran into him at the grocery store and he was actually off tonight."

Ted took a long drink from his glass of beer and set it down. "I'm sure it will be a wonderful party, dear. Are you going to wear those jeans?"

I looked at my watch. "Yikes, I gotta get changed. I won't be long." I ran to the bedroom and surveyed my closet. I pulled out a long full skirt made of sown together silk scarves that I had found at a market in Seattle when I was with Holly. I quickly took off my jeans and sweater, and slipped on the skirt, a matching sky blue sleeveless blouse and, for a touch of playfulness, a sequin and feather stretchy headband, and some dangly crystal earrings. I even grabbed a blue feather boa Holly and I had got when we were in New Orleans. We both loved to travel and hear jazz, and our husbands weren't interested. We always had such fun. I dabbed on some fresh lipstick, and added colour to my cheeks and eyelids. I decided against the high heels and found some sequins-covered ballet slippers.

When I came back into the living room, Ted beamed at me. "You're gorgeous. I didn't know a woman could change so quickly."

"I don't like to waste too much time on that sort of thing. You know, Ted, I was just thinking about our conversation. I don't think I'm trying to make *you* like me."

"That's because you know I do, and I admire and respect you."

I leaned down and gave him a kiss. "Oh, there's the doorbell. Wish me luck."

Holly and Kathy were at the back door with their husbands even though the couples had come in separate cars. Perhaps, they were as nervous as I was and planned to make their entrance at the same time. I took their coats and found them drinks, and then led them to meet Ted. Ted had his feet up in the old blue chair and greeted them in a relaxed manner.

The front doorbell rang and I was thrilled to open the door to Joey and Di. The fact that Joey and I had hung out together on a number of band stands made us kindred spirits. After all, we had been a part of some important and unusual occasions together; from the swearing in of politicians, to dances, to funerals, to festivals. And because we played jazz, we shared in the ups and downs of improvising. When it was good, it felt divine, and when it was uninspired, it was just notes.

I felt the warmth of a true friend as Joey gave me a hug. Diana was looking radiant with her long curly hair and flawless skin. She was excited to be out with her man, as such opportunities rarely presented themselves with all the gigs Joey played.

"I'm so glad you just live up the road, Jan. We can have a few drinks and relax," said Joey.

"I bet you'd both like a scotch, eh?" I said, tossing their coats on the coat rack. I took them in to meet everyone and went in the kitchen to get the drinks – one neat and one with water. While there, I poured myself a generous glass of undiluted merlot and had a swallow to calm myself before heading back in.

The men were asking Joey about Tennessee. His southern drawl always surprised people. I put on some background music and soon, we were caught up in a swirl of animated conversation. All except Ted. When Keith asked him if he was managing to paint most days, he gave a polite answer and didn't ask any questions in return, even though I had told him Keith was a prize-winning artist. I felt a little anxious about his lack of involvement but he seemed content to rest in his chair nursing his Guinness and observing.

I jumped up to get a tray of appetizers and offered it to each person. I noticed that Mark and Keith avoided eye contact with me as they thanked me for cheese, crackers and veggies.

I wasn't able to get involved in most of the topics, since I was popping back and forth to the kitchen, refreshing drinks, and staying focused on the timing of the various courses.

Kathy came out to offer a hand. She was one of the few people I had confided in when the marriage was floundering. Her counselling skills and lack of judgement had been a god-send. She also understood how difficult this current transition was. I smiled and assured her it was all easy, and told her to go enjoy herself.

I took the spine out of the fish, placed the salmon on the platter with fresh dill and lemon, and put the vegetables and rice in serving bowls. Returning to the living room, I found there was a rowdy discussion going on about the latest gaffe the politicians had made. They now allowed trees to be cut down when old houses were torn down, so that new houses could cover a much bigger footprint. Since I didn't own a house anymore, I felt somewhat removed from their passion and instead squatted beside Ted's chair. "We're going to eat in a few minutes. Would you like to be at the head of the table?" I pointed to the chair that was just a few feet from his chair, as the dining table was in the living room. "I'll bring you a plate with everything on it but I'm going to let everyone else get their own."

Ted patted my arm and said, "Lovely, dear. I'm glad you'll be sitting down soon."

Interrupting the others, I told everyone to come in and help themselves in the kitchen.

Food and wine relieve any tension, and it felt like old times as we toasted to new beginnings and settled into a delicious meal with animated conversation and laughter. I looked around and felt happy that everyone seemed to be enjoying themselves, and even Ted was smiling at something Di was saying. I was sitting at the opposite end but we grinned at each other and he gave me the thumbs up.

I suddenly remembered that I had left one of the salads in the fridge so I went to each person and urged them to try some. Once again, I was uncomfortably aware of Mark and Keith's coolness. I understood they had an issue with me, but I wondered why they had accepted the invitation. Perhaps, their wives had forced them to come.

I had hardly touched my meal but I looked at Joey's plate and started to giggle.

"Joey, go get some more."

"Goodness, gracious me. It was wonderful. I couldn't slow down, but I'm afraid I must now. Why aren't you eating?"

"Maybe you could help me with mine. I'll probably really enjoy the leftovers tomorrow but I think I'll play the piano for a bit to change the mood. Feel free to come and play some bass lines."

The piano filled the dining room and I was able to survey the crowded living room as I relaxed into the keys. I set up a Latin rhythm and played *You Don't Know What Love Is*. Those minor keys were my favourite these days. To my surprise, Joey sat beside me on the piano stool when I brought it to an end. He put his scotch on the side table.

"Why don't you swing it? I like the way you do, *'Sometimes I'm Happy'*."

Even though he was a bit tipsy, he supported me with a swinging walking bass on the piano and I sang the verse. *Sometimes I'm happy, sometimes I'm blue. My disposition depends on you.* While I was improvising on it, I said, "Joey, here we are on a night off. Thank you for doing this."

Joey started laughing as he said, "I'm murdering this. I'm sure not a pianist."

"But it's so fun. What is it about playing music with a buddy?"

Only Ted was listening to us. The conversation was a boisterous backdrop to our duet. My friends were used to me playing during get-togethers. If I was honest with myself, I was better at entertaining than partying.

I gave Joey a squeeze and got up to clear plates and sort out the dessert. When Ted came out of the washroom, he sat on a kitchen stool, and praised my food and asked me if I was okay.

"Thank you for asking, Ted," I said, giving him a hug. "You're such a sweetheart. Look at this beautiful torte."

"Did you actually make that?"

"Do you know my uncle gave me the recipe for this? It's really easy."

"The musician?"

"No, his brother. He was a social worker. He and his wife also adopted kids. He knows I love chocolate. And so do you. How about a cup of tea?"

"Love one. I wish I could help you."

"You are helping me just by being here. I feel like I'm stronger and more confident than I would be if I was doing this alone." I poured the boiling water into a big tea pot. "Ted, I know this isn't really your kind of thing but I'm so glad you're here."

"Oh, so am I. I'm not getting too involved in the conversations but I like to sit back and observe, as you know."

I was concentrating on getting some dishes into the dishwasher so that I had space for the dessert and tea, but I was still curious. "Did you come to any conclusions from your observations?"

"You need to relax and trust yourself a little more."

"Oh darn, am I still trying too hard?"

"Yes. People have a very strong opinion about adultery and yet, it happens all the time. Perhaps, that is why the opinions are so strong. Do you mind if I ask you, what happened to the guy that caused all this?"

"Oh, he doesn't even live here. I think his role was just to make me see how much I was missing by pretending I was married. I shall always be grateful to him for that."

My buddy, Holly, walked into the kitchen and said, "We wondered where you were. The food was fabulous. What are you talking about?"

"I *will* tell you sometime, but right now, help me take these into the other room."

We enjoyed the dessert and were about to have another drink when Ted said, "Is anyone going home my way, by chance?"

Mark said, "Of course, Ted, we'll take you home."

Within ten minutes, everyone had left. I looked at my watch. It was 9:15. I wondered why Ted couldn't have taken a taxi. I looked at the dirty dishes, pots and pans, and furniture that would have to be rearranged and I started to laugh. I would be more inclined to cry if I hadn't had that last conversation with Ted. He made me realize it was time to stop trying to relive the good times I had had with my husband. Perhaps, I would lose some friends while I was at it, but life is ever changing. Professor Ted would likely help me to understand this more, I thought, as I took off my boa to start scrubbing. I poured myself another glass of wine and began to sing *Sometimes I'm Happy, sometimes I'm blue...*

Hanging Out with Musicians

"Ted, why did you have a tray sent up for your meal. Aren't you well?" I asked.

"Of course, I'm well. I'm not going to eat with those ijits every day. It's exhausting. I want a real conversation, not the same question asked of me every two minutes."

Ted had been moved to a Care Facility called Sunrise, and the sign outside said, 'Long Term Care for Memory Loss and Dementia'. I felt like I qualified for this more than Ted, who was embarrassed to be labelled in this way. Since he needed more care than Carlton House was able to give him, I presumed this must have been the only one that was available when he was moved.

"You know, Janet," Ted continued, "there is only one chap I don't mind spending a bit of time with, but he's a lost cause in the evening because his daughter keeps him supplied with beer. And he really can't handle it."

"Oh, you mean Joseph. Does he ever preach at you? Being a retired Minister I thought—"

"Not in the slightest. I think that's why they put him in here. He doesn't believe half the things he was forced to preach about."

I walked around, folding clean clothes that were in a laundry basket and tossing out old food in his fridge. "My only concern, Ted, is that this place stipulates that you have to be well enough to make it down for meals on your own, even if it's in a wheelchair. And you can do it with your cane. So, if you keep requiring trays up here, you will likely be put in a total nursing care residence. That will be much worse – chances are, everyone will be a gibbering idiot."

"I've thought of that." Ted lifted the heavy book beside him and flipped pages to look at photos taken of outer space from the eye of Hubble. "And, I *am* going to my exercise class daily because I don't want to get so weak, I can't lift a tea cup. I just wish this bloody knee worked." He put the book back and rubbed his knee as he gazed out the window. "Oh, look at those birds soaring and playing together," he said, changing moods suddenly. "I just love being up here above the trees watching the birds."

"It is a beautiful view, Ted. And being so close to Beacon Hill Park, you'd never know you were in the city." I smiled as I watched his furrowed brow relax and his eyes shine with enthusiasm behind the rimless glasses that were hanging off the end of his nose.

"Yes, I'm very grateful. I love sitting in this big chair going over my memories." He looked over at the small totem pole sitting on the floor by the table that was loaded with unopened mail. "I often fall asleep and create new things in my dreams. Those birds are so entertaining."

"Maybe you could emote about birds for me?" I suggested, reaching for my journal and pen.

I had no sooner put pen to paper than Ted was speaking slowly, as he stared out the window.

Birds

The sky is full of magic – the magic of birds.

Crows, black and active, flying onto telephone poles, wires and chimney tops. Their ceaseless activity keeps me amused. Sometimes they fight and sometimes they cooperate with other crows, and share things like scraps.

However, along come the gulls – pure white. I see their wings gleaming in the distance and then they approach and glide past the window like gentle spirits. Gulls shriek a lot. They shriek and scream as they float above the houses.

However, their real home is by the sea and there they are masters of the environment.

How did the medieval people see birds before mankind discovered the magic of flight? They gave angels wings because they could fly from heaven down to earth and would appear as wondrous creatures. Then, man invented ways to fly and now he surpasses the speed of sound, and you cannot be graceful with wings of that speed.

Watching birds in flight calms the mind and fills you with wonder even though they are relatively commonplace. We take them for granted and yet, if we jumped from the rooftop with our arms outstretched, we would land with a thud. We lack the grace of flight but humans try to capture it in ballet and dance. Dancers leap across the stage balancing on tiptoe and trying, with infinite skill, to imitate the birds.

Yet, one of my favourite birds is the hen. I love to eat a roast chicken and boil an egg. If I purchase a dozen eggs, it will give me breakfast for a week. So, while watching the birds outside fly with infinite grace, I can sit and eat the one that doesn't fly, and yet provides me with sustenance. Two of my favourite creatures are birds and pigs. Together, they make for a hearty breakfast. Bacon and eggs are Nature's food. Pigs can't fly but they do provide us with a heavenly sustenance.

Birds can be quite poetic and colourful. They amaze us with their beauty and they gossip together like bored housewives chattering at the street end. Life would be dull without their presence.

I finished writing just as someone knocked on the door. A beautiful girl, with thick dark hair and perfect olive skin, wearing a pale-yellow uniform, stood at the open door and apologized when she saw me. "Hello, Ted, I have your pills, but I can come back later to get you ready for bed. I didn't know you had company." She smiled at me and gave Ted the small cup of smashed pills with water. "Are you his daughter?" she asked shyly.

"No, we're just good buddies," I said, enjoying her lovely smile and gentleness. I looked at her name tag. "Francie, what kind of pills does he have there? Are they for sleeping?"

She laughed. "Ted doesn't need help sleeping. You sleep too much, Ted," she teased, brushing her hand down his arm before taking the cup and putting it in the garbage. "Ted is lucky. He doesn't need many pills compared to others. Just the ones for Parkinson's to help with shaking, and ones for his blood pressure, although his blood pressure is very good for his age." Turning back to Ted, she said, "I'll come back later to put you to bed."

"Good, make it *much* later please."

She smiled and closed the door quietly behind her.

"What a sweetheart," said Ted. "And do you know they even put baby powder on my bottom after my bath. At first, I was embarrassed but I just love those girls."

"I'm so glad, Ted. I know you aren't totally happy with being here but you sure know how to look on the bright side." I started singing, "*Grey skies are going to clear up. Put on a Happy Face.*"

"What are you doing tonight, love? Would you like to go over to Ken's restaurant for a decent spicy meal? I haven't seen him in so long. God, I hate the bland meals here."

"I'm sorry, Ted, I didn't bring my car. I just walked over tonight now that you're living closer to me, and I'm going to go from here to the Vista 18 to hear my friends play music."

"Please take me. Get me out of here!"

I fidgeted a bit, wondering how I could leave him like this. "It's a long three blocks uphill – I wouldn't be able to push your wheelchair. Mind you, it would be interesting coming home."

Ted slumped in his chair. He stared fixedly at the self-portrait by his friend Arthur Shilling of the Ojibwa clan.

"Listen, Ted, do you think you could use your self-motorized wheel-chair? I know you haven't used it in a while and I've never tried it."

"Of course, I can."

"Okay. We'll have to sneak out the back door. I don't think I can sign you out this late at night."

"It's only 8:00. Bloody hell, it's a jail here."

"Let's do it," I said decisively, throwing my shoulders back and rummaging through his closet. "This jacket is lovely, and the tweed cap and red scarf. Hmmm – we need gloves – any idea where you keep them?"

"I can't help you. Someone always helps me dress these days."

I opened drawers but only found neatly folded undergarments, gym pants, T-shirts and … "Oh good, help me get this sweater on you."

Ted eagerly obliged as I rushed to put the thick white knit over his head. We struggled to get his arm in the right hole.

"There's a technique to this, eh?"

I brought over the wheelchair after finally managing to get his jacket on and throwing the scarf around his neck. We were both hot.

"I'm sorry about the gloves, Ted. It's cold out there and you'll be driving so you can't put your hands in your pockets."

"No problem," said Ted, hoisting himself into the chair, which I had forgotten to brake. He teetered precariously as the chair veered off to the left.

Finally, he was in and looking so darn proud of himself. I threw on my coat, slung my purse over my shoulder and opened the door for Ted. He ran into the wall and laughed hysterically.

"I have to get used to this thing again."

The elevator doors opened and we went down to the main floor. I went ahead, signalling Ted to follow me towards the back door. Probably I didn't need to sneak around like this but I knew Ted would enjoy the adventure. I put my finger to my lips and Ted's eyes sparkled with glee. There was a sing-along going on in the main hall but hopefully, they wouldn't notice us sneaking past the large opening. Ted hated those sing-alongs.

We were nearly to the door when an officious looking woman wearing a badge came out of a side room and stood in front of me.

"Hello, you two – where might you be going?"

"Oh, Hello, Luv," I said, picking up Ted's mannerisms. "We're just going out to the garden before it's completely dark. Ted loves being outside as you probably know."

"We haven't seen much of him today. That's a good idea. He could use the air. There aren't too many flowers out there, of course, but the heather and greens are nice. The rain has stopped. Ring the bell when you're ready to come in."

"Of course. Thank you, ma'am."

As soon as the door closed behind us, I said, "Okay, Ted, follow me."

Ted used the lever on the chair to manoeuvre the narrow path, only careening into the garden a couple of times. Each time he gave a toothy guffaw. Once we were outside the gate on the sidewalk, it was a little easier, although the roads were busy. We waited for the light to change in the damp fog, and Ted eyed the couple beside us. They had numerous piercings, and even tattoos on their faces and necks. The girl gave him a dazzling smile, which Ted returned.

We continued up the hill, with me silently cheering him on. I knew his hands must be freezing but he wasn't complaining. I prayed there was enough juice in the battery to get us there and back.

"See that big building ahead? We're going to the eighteenth floor."

"Yippee," shouted Ted. An elegant gentleman wearing a long, brown woolen coat and carrying a leather briefcase tipped his fedora as he passed.

After being greeted at the entrance of the hotel by a dapper doorman, we found the bank of elevators. We rode up and before reaching the top, we could hear the music and smell the aroma of spicy food coming down the elevator shaft. Ted gasped when the doors opened.

My buddy, Al, was playing guitar and his friend, Bryn, was singing as he held his trumpet. I didn't know who the sexy bass player was. God, I should have married a bass player, not my Tai Chi teacher. Ah well, we had several good years together, and I was less lonely now riding solo than when I was in the marriage.

The floor to ceiling windows displayed the silhouette of the snow-capped mountains to the south and the twinkling lights of the city below. I directed Ted to the only available table where a wheelchair could easily fit. It seemed to be waiting for us. Al looked up with a flash of surprise and a huge grin.

After getting Ted settled and playfully checking his hands for frostbite, I asked him what he would like to drink. Expecting Guinness, I was surprised when he leaned back with a debonair wave of his hand and said, "A gin and tonic, please."

"Ted, when did you last have a gin and tonic?"

"Oh, it's been years. Mind you, my memory isn't so good!" he said with sarcasm. "Occasionally, Nicky and I would have one, sitting in the screened-in porch, on a rare warm evening. Needed that screening with all the black flies."

"You must be talking about the Yukon, or do they have those in New Zealand?"

"I was thinking about our rustic cabin on Crag Lake. I'd love to show it to you someday. I've donated it for artists to use, but of course, I can go anytime. Wouldn't that be fun?" he said before taking a small sip from the straw.

"How do you organize the artists that want to use it?"

"The Foundation Barry helped me set up is called THARS which stands for the Ted Harrison Artist Retreat Society. It allows artists to live there for several months to further develop their talents." He turned and watched the band intently, tapping his fingers on the table in time with the beat.

Bryn announced that they were taking a short break and were going to visit the famous artist, Ted Harrison.

People clapped and looked over at our table with curiosity and delight. Soon, Al and Bryn had pulled up chairs, and several people crowded around the table to tell Ted how much his work meant to them. I watched to see if this was annoying or exhausting for Ted but he was relaxed and seemed to bask in the attention. Once again, I felt a sadness, knowing how alienated Ted was in his lonely existence, living with strangers who didn't stimulate him. I reminded myself that he enjoyed his caregivers who were from many different countries, and they obviously appreciated him.

The bass player brought over a chair and squeezed in beside Al. Al said, "Hey, Jason, have you met Jan before? She's a dynamite jazz pianist."

Jason stretched across to shake my hand. "Hi, Jan. I understand you're from Ontario too."

"Yes, but aren't we lucky to call this home? I'm glad I got to hear you. Victoria can never have too many good bass players."

Ted eyed me curiously as I relaxed with my fellow musicians. He turned to Al and said, "Do you happen to know the *Romance d'Amour*? I know it's usually played on a classical guitar. I loved hearing Leona Boyd play it."

"Yes, that was one of the first tunes I learned. The writer is not known, just that he or she is a 19th Century composer from Spain."

"Al is a walking dictionary on all sorts of music – especially the Beatles," I told Ted.

A man sitting at the bar came over and stood beside Ted. "So sorry to interrupt, sir – my name is Andre. I had to share that I am lucky enough to own one of your paintings. And it has lifted my mood for years. It's one with coloured horses running across a Ted landscape."

"Ah yes – I do love the power of horses stampeding."

"When you live with something so personal, you feel you know the artist. Therefore, I was interested to read about the many changes you've been through lately. That must have been a challenge to move from your home, and to stop painting."

Ted laughed. "Change is good because it's in keeping with the truth of life. That's why Buddhist monks make sand mandalas and then destroy them. Ultimately, we must part with everything, so we shouldn't get attached to anything."

"Easier said than done," said Jason. "I've got a love/hate relationship with my car. My wallet wishes I would part with it."

"What have you got?" asked Ted.

"A 67 E-Type Jag."

"Oh, those are so pretty."

"When they're running, yes. Did you ever get into cars?"

"No, I'm practical when it comes to vehicles. But the most fun I had was on a motorcycle. I rode off and on over the years. It's very stimulating to be moving with the elements, free of a container. I could smell fresh mown fields and feel the wind, and could almost touch the birds flying past. I even liked the roar of the engine under me. In those days, they were pretty loud."

I pictured Ted dressed in leather, helmet and goggles, following the curve of a mountain, alone, but never lonely.

The rest of the table had been silently fixated on the conversation. Bryn suddenly said, "C'mon, boys. It's time to get back for our next set."

"We'll be listening," said Ted. "I'm enjoying your music – it's mostly my era."

"Thank you, Mr. Harrison," said Bryn. "It was an honour to meet you."

"Andre put his hand on Ted's shoulder and said, "It certainly was," before turning back to the bar.

"Oh, by the way," I called to the boys. "Don't be surprised if we leave soon. Ted isn't supposed to be out so we need to sneak back in through the garage."

The music started and Ted sipped on the straw in his tall glass. He wrinkled his nose. "God, I don't know what anyone sees in these drinks."

"Don't feel you have to drink it, Ted. They'll have your warm milk waiting when you crawl into bed."

"Yes, another benefit to the place." After listening to the music and watching the musicians, he said, "I like your friends – especially Al."

I paid the bill and worked to get Ted's coat on. A woman sitting at the next table leapt up to help.

"Wow, that seemed easy for you."

"I used to be a nurse," she explained. She shook Ted's hand. "It's a pleasure to meet you, sir. You came to our kids' school when they were young and you had a big influence on them. One is now a graphic designer and the other is a poet. You are a gifted teacher."

"I'm so glad to hear that. Give them my best, will you?" asked Ted, pushing his cap on a jaunty angle. He made sure the scarf was crossed securely.

Before the doors of the elevator closed on us, Al mouthed "Bye" and I blew a kiss.

Ted sighed and said, "Janet, I so enjoyed that. And I liked the way your friends treated me like a normal person. I get tired of people asking the same questions about my art."

"Well, Ted, seeing the response tonight, I certainly see how popular you are."

Ted maneuvered his chair out the glass doors of the building and breathed in the damp cool night air with relish. The streets were deserted, apart from a cab hoping for a fare. We crossed to the wide sidewalk and Ted laughed giddily as he steered, none too straight, down the hill. "Almost as much fun as riding a motorcycle."

I jogged behind him warning him to be ready for the stoplight coming up.

As we waited for the light to change, I crouched beside him and rubbed his hands. "I love you, Ted."

"I adore you, Pet. I wish I could do this kind of thing every night. No wonder you enjoy being a musician. My art has been very solitary."

"So is practising piano, believe me." As we continued towards his brightly lit building, I said, "Hey, Ted, do you happen to know the pass code for your Parkade?"

"Let me think – is it 4872 or 2748. Since I don't have a car anymore, I rarely use it."

I tried various combinations to no avail. "Darn, I've got it written down in my other purse. I'll have to ring security I'm afraid."

"I was admiring that purse. Looks well made. And I love the blue."

"Thanks, Ted, got it in Uruguay at an outdoor market. Trust you to notice."

"Yes," said the curt voice through the speaker.

"Hello. It's Jan and I've got Ted down here with me, and we've forgotten the code."

"All right. Stand back."

As we watched the large door rumble open, I said, "So much for sneaking in. Let's be cool."

We had to take the elevator to the main floor in order to get to the elevators for the rooms. The head Matron, wearing a jacket and badge, and Francie, Ted's favourite aide were standing at the guest desk waiting for us.

"What is the meaning of this? You didn't sign Ted out and we were worried about him. We are responsible for him, and in his condition, he could easily wander. We were about to phone the police." She studied Ted carefully and her tense expression softened slightly when she gazed into Ted's smiling, round face.

"Don't blame Janet. I was starving when we were out in the garden and we thought we'd have a little snack somewhere. And do you know what? I'm still hungry! Have you got a chicken leg or something to go with my milk?"

"Francie, take Ted to his room immediately."

I leaned down to kiss Ted good night. "That was great fun, Ted. I'll see you soon."

"Yes, Darling, please come back soon. You've cheered me immensely."

After they had moved down the hall, the woman gave me a studied look. "Be careful, my dear, or you won't be allowed to visit Ted again. That has happened to several of Ted's acquaintances already."

"What? Can you do that?"

"It's not my decision, I'm afraid. But it's understandable. There are always people wanting things from Ted and he is unable to say no."

"Is that why he hardly has any visitors? He's going mad with boredom."

"There is a certain procedure we must follow in order to stay in business."

"Of course. Well, thank you so much for being so understanding," I said. "Ted and I really need each other."

I thought about what I had just said as I walked up the leafy, peaceful street towards my apartment. We really did need and understand each other. We loved our solitary times and our positive friends, but somehow, we could totally relax with each other. Laughter and tears were common visitors when we got together. I pictured him riding down the hill, the red scarf waving behind him, and I smiled.

Sex, Sin and Creativity

I nervously entered the front door of Sunrise the following week, wondering if I was in trouble for taking Ted out to the bar without signing him out. It *had* been irresponsible of me. However, the girl at the front desk was very friendly when I signed myself in.

Joseph waved to me from the lounge and I stopped briefly to chat with him. He was sitting alone in a room full of empty couches and chairs.

"Anything new happening today, Joseph?" I asked.

"I'm afraid Ted hasn't been in top form the last few days."

"Really, what's going on?" I knew Joseph liked to dramatize life – I'm sure I would be the same if I was as confined as he was. "He doesn't have a phone anymore so I can't talk to him every day like I used to."

"I know the doctor was in to see him. It might be a bit of influenza. Quite a few people have had it here. Personally, I think he's depressed."

"Joseph, I notice you seem to stay positive and curious about life. What's your secret?"

"I just take every day with gratitude. And my daughter looks after me well."

"And you still enjoy reading, I see."

An elderly woman came through from the hallway pushing her walker and mumbling, "Where is my baby?"

I felt helpless as I watched her but Joseph ignored her and said, "The library here has a few good books in it." He held up a heavy hardcover with shaky arms. "This is about the Second World War. I never get tired of reading about it for some reason."

"My Dad is the same, even though he dodged the action by building ships for the Navy in Newfoundland."

"I dodged it too – for health reasons – and yet, I'm still somewhat functioning sixty years later."

I laughed, shook his hand, and took the elevator to Ted's top-floor room.

Ted looked up and gave a weak smile. "Hello, Dear. It seems like ages since I've seen you."

"I had a gig on Gabriola Island so I stayed up there for a few days and took a course at the Haven."

"What kind of course?"

"It's called Coming Alive."

"Hah, sounds like something I should take, not you. Was it interesting?"

"It was pretty emotional, actually. I don't know why I keep doing this to myself." I felt Ted's head as I leaned down to kiss him on the cheek. "Are you feeling okay? Joseph was saying there's a bug going around."

"Oh, the doctor said it's nothing. I just missed you, I guess. We had such fun last time I saw you. It's been very dull ever since."

"Have you gone out on the bus with the others to see the sights? You used to like doing that."

"No, the weather is a bit gloomy."

"Maybe I should do some Quantum Healing on you."

"You mean Reiki? You haven't done that in ages. I would love it if you'd give me some energy."

I sat down on the floor in front of him. "They say QT is like Reiki on steroids."

"How do you mean?"

"It's the same basic principle of using the hands and getting the ego out of the way to let the Universal Energy come through. They call it Supercharging. Do you mind if I practise on you? I've only been doing it for a few months."

"I wish you would," said Ted. "I'm just watching the sky change. I still find that very entertaining."

"It's a good meditation. I'm going to put you more upright, if you don't mind." While squatting on the floor in front of him, I explained. "I'm putting a finger in each ear to measure if the sphenoid/occipital bones are unbalanced, thus causing weakness." I eyed the line across both fingers. "You're crooked, Ted. We'll see if the right side goes down when I'm done. Did you ever have a concussion, or was your birth difficult?"

"Probably, I can't remember."

I got behind Ted's chair and placing my hands in various places on his head, I concentrated, imagining I was sweeping energy up my legs and from my heart to my hands.

"Wow, your hands are hot. What are you doing?"

"I'm using my imagination – you know all about that. I've got a beautiful coloured cyclone of energy moving into your body and my heart is the channel. Give me a few minutes. But let me know if you feel any discomfort."

"This is so relaxing. It's like a warm wind, and I think my eyes are changing." Ted took his glasses off.

I focused all my attention for a few minutes. Then, I came around to measure the line between his ears. It was straight. "Lovely, Ted. I'm just going to do this in a few different spots and end on your knee. Do you want some music on?"

"No, thanks. This is perfect."

I worked my way down the various chakras as best I could in the lazy boy recliner. Ted lay quietly with his eyes closed, now and then sighing. Then, I sat on the floor and ran energy into his knee. I knew he'd had a fall when he was out hiking years before and that's why he was so lame.

Ted said, "Let me feel your hands for a minute."

I reached up and we held hands. Ted's hands were warm and as soft as a baby.

"Amazing. Your hands are usually cool. You can practise on me anytime. You know, that gave my knee some relief."

"Thanks, Ted, for being so open minded about it. That's the key. People that are cynical don't get any results."

"How did you get involved in that?"

"The Quantum Touch teacher was giving a demonstration at a church in James Bay and a friend asked me to come with him to see it. We were at the back of the room, yet, the teacher asked me to come to the front so he could demonstrate. He had me turn my back to the audience and he showed that one hip was higher than the other. I agreed that I was born with scoliosis. So he ran energy for maybe five minutes on my hips and everything straightened out. One leg is no longer shorter and all my clothes fit now. I knew I had to learn how to do that so I signed up for the course. I've now taken three courses with him."

"So what do you think is the key?"

"You, of all people, know how powerful imagination is. And I learned so much about it, first of all, by being raised in Christian Science, and seeing many healings that happened simply by trusting that we are always loved and supported by something we can't see. I can feel that God presence if I just stop thinking so much. Why is that such a challenge?"

Ted laughed. "I seem to be an expert at it."

I continued to explain, even though I didn't really want to discuss my marriage. "I experienced some profound things during my marriage of eighteen years. He was a Tai Chi Master who learned how to toss people around without using muscle. His Chinese Master, Henry, would come to Victoria for the weekend about once a month and they took delight in throwing each other across the living room into a couch while I was cooking in the kitchen. Henry wouldn't even touch Ray to do it. I really wanted to learn how to do it. The funny thing is that once Ray learned how, he stopped teaching. Perhaps, he understood then why it was considered a secret that could only be entrusted to a few. I don't think Henry expected Ray would learn to do it but he practised in his studio endlessly."

"Well, it seems like you're putting what you learned to good use."

"I seem to always be searching and I'm not sure why. I don't think I intend to be a healer but I am fascinated by energy, and I'm always curious about anything like that," I said.

Ted pondered for a bit. "Have you studied tantric sex?"

I laughed. "Need you ask? My ex-husband and I studied Mantak Chia's method which is called the Tao of Love.

During the years we practised it, we were madly in love. It was only when we got away from that practise that we realized we had very little in common."

"So why didn't you keep doing it?"

"I don't think we realized all of that at the time. For one thing, his Master told him it wasn't good for us. Said it would drain the energy. And yet, we were both energized, and I felt very creative and relaxed."

Ted said, "One of the dangers of following a Master is you stop thinking for yourself."

I thought about all the different religions I had studied, and workshops I had taken. "Is that always the case?"

"Sure, look at all the dysfunctional religions. Perhaps, your husband was selfish if he let you get so unhappy."

"Ted, I'm no angel, believe me. Relationship problems are never caused by just one person. But I will say, I didn't feel seen by him. That's why I feel so good with you – you get me."

"Janet, I'd like to write a poem that's a little different than what we've done before."

"Really?" I asked, as I reached for my journal.

"Yes, I'm going to use my imagination while I think of you."

"This should be interesting. Fire away," I said.

Ted seemed to go into a dream state as he shut his eyes and slowly spoke.

Sex Appeal

I gaze upon your body and my fingers tingle with suppressed anticipation. I would love to trace a line through the valley of your breasts and feel the delightful smooth waist, which speaks to me from under a mass of clothing. Those gentle soft nipples grow hard with desire and point the way to Nirvana. Gradually, you grow limp under my touch and you dream of exotic desires.

Next to a beautiful meal, sex is the hors d'oeuvre or probably the supreme climax to an evening of bliss. With food, wine and sex, what else can one wish for? Your delightful kisses give visions of other delights which await but now appear distant as the far horizon.

To love someone is not only to know them, but also to feel that they are a part of you and that their beauty is not only an inner beauty but has an exterior form too. I float along with visions of holding you in my arms, enjoying each minute of our closeness.

I set the book down and met Ted's eyes. "Ted, I gotta say that makes me a little uncomfortable."

"Why? We were talking about imagination. I was using mine and I enjoyed it immensely." He had an impish smile on his face.

I burst out laughing. "You little devil. Ted, I'm flattered, and I'm thrilled you're still so passionate. Listen, would you be interested in meeting one of my older students? She lost her husband a few years ago and she's still got it. She's from Ireland, has a great sense of humour, and I just love her."

"If you like her, then yes, I would like to meet her. As long as she's capable of an intelligent conversation, let's all go for lunch. And as long as she's not uptight about sin."

"What?"

"Grab your pen, my dear."

Sin

I like sin because it is forbidden. It's considered bad by many people who don't know how to have a good time. Sin is closely related to sex – that is, in the Christian calendar. But we Hindus don't worry about that and so we are rather freer in our actions.

There's nothing worse than having a God who is behind you all the time, and looking at what you do and judging you. The least sign of any enjoyment must be nipped in the bud if one is seeking joy. We are expected to be puritanical with grim faces and grim habits. The habits must conform to a rigid formula of purity and sanctity, which one doesn't feel. But apparently, it pleases others to feel that way and they have decided that all mankind should tame their ardours and become unsmiling, virtuous nonentities.

There is no reason to go overboard but there is no reason why we should not jump the ship occasionally and swim in the broad ocean of warm delight. If we have to stick to the puritanical ways of priests and nuns, why did God bother to make women beautiful and men attracted to them? It is a law of nature that this attraction should be part of the enjoyment of life or else, we become frightened of being ourselves or frightened of breaking a rule which is not written down but is taken for granted by 'good people'.

It is best to paddle one's canoe into the more boisterous passages of the river so that there is a rush of blood through the system, and the journey becomes much more exciting and enjoyable.

So, farewell, Puritans. I leave your shores and venture out into the open oceans of desire.

Ted closed his eyes and rested his chin on his hands. I watched him for a few minutes and then pulled on my coat. He opened his eyes and said, "Must you go?"

"I'll be back, Ted. I've got an early bird student tomorrow."

"Of course, dear. But I was just thinking – perhaps we could do one more while we're on this subject?"

"You mean sex?"

"No! Get your mind out of the gutter."

Creativity

God created the world in seven days but man has created since the beginning of his time on earth and will continue to create well into the future. All the materials used in forming art are wondrous in the results they procure. Paintings, drawings and sculpture can make us weep or cry with ecstasy. Each work of art has its individual influence on the person who views it and the results are as changeable as humanity itself.

It is a world continually being explored by the human mind and hand. Artists launch into the unknown and find gems of creation greater in their individuality than the real gems mined from the earth. The range of creativity is a vast hinterland of the mind, which transcends time and changes its face through the ages.

The world may have been created in seven days but man will create through the millenniums of existence.

I tucked the journal in my purse and stood up. "Thanks, Ted, for that. And especially for helping me with my healing homework."

"Thank you, dear. I feel so much better than before you arrived. Please come back as soon as you can. You do know that I would never hurt you, don't you?"

"Ted, you couldn't hurt a flea. I like that you're so open about your feelings to me. I just don't want to give you the wrong impression when I tell you I love you."

"Of course. You don't have to explain anything to me. We are connected in so many beautiful ways and when I enjoy myself with someone – which isn't all that often – I want it to continue."

I leaned down and kissed Ted just as Francie walked in to help him with his nightly ablutions.

Ross Bay Cemetery

I parked the car in front of the old farmhouse that had been converted into three suites. "Ted, are you sure you can make it up all these stairs? Last time we were here, Barry was with us to help you up."

"Of course, I can," said Ted. "Wouldn't miss it for the world."

I had moved to the main floor of the farmhouse, across from Ross Bay Cemetery with a view to the ocean. I was so happy to be back in my old neighbourhood. The wind blew through the cracks, I was never warm, the tenants above and below were noisy, the kitchen and plumbing were primitive, but I loved the high ceilings, the wood floors, and large windows that framed a glorious view. My neighbours preferred my piano to the noisy family that used to live there before me.

There was a heavy-duty railing for Ted to hold onto and he patiently hoisted himself up one leg at a time while I did very little, except encourage him from behind.

"What are we eating tonight?" asked Ted. He had stopped part-way up to catch his breath.

"Grandma's pot roast."

"I hope it isn't that old," chuckled Ted as he forced himself to the landing.

I unlocked the door and took him directly into the kitchen to sit, cranking the heat up as I stashed our coats in the closet. It was a cool November day. I put some mellow Stan Getz on in the background. Since I used to play alto sax years before, I appreciated hearing it played with feeling.

"Is it a red wine night with the beef?" I asked.

"Why don't you have that? I know it's your preference but if you've got a Guinness, I'm craving one."

I passed the can and a tall glass to him, and watched him gaze at the creamy suds with a blissful smile on his face as he filled it. I brought my glass of zinfandel over and we clinked glasses.

"Have we written about Guinness yet?" he asked.

"No, that should have been our first subject." I sat down at the kitchen table facing towards the sea, and pulled my notebook over from the big window sill. Ted lifted his glass to his lips and drank, leaving his moustache snowier than ever. He waited for me to find a pen and then he began to speak:

Guinness

I wearily crawled back to my room. The hard day of work and weather had dulled my soul. I had encountered numerous people. Many were touched with desperation and frustration with the tenor of life. Each person's problem stole a piece of my energy until my body seemed empty, dull and dry. However, in the fridge there sat my salvation – a large can of Irish Guinness.

I clicked it open and the creamy suds poured out into a glass. This reminded me of life on earth being created. The boiling, bubbly, creamy head rose to the surface from the dark interior of the body of the liquid. I admired its colour before tasting the first wonderful draft. Immediately, my spirits rose like the creamy head of the liquid to the surface and my imagination soared with each sip. Surely, this was the nectar of the gods. No wine could match its delicacy and subtle flavour. I drank it to the last dregs, and found all my tensions had disappeared and my mind was becalmed after a stormy sea. Oh, that such liquor could have such a positive effect upon the mind.

I sipped it slowly so that the delightful feeling would last longer. But alas, like everything in life that's good and happy, it was finished, leaving me with a blessed memory. Oh, Ireland, Ireland, that charming green land has given birth to this glorious liquid. I could hear the angels singing praises to Guinness from fleecy clouds with the sun bursting through like the creamy head.

However, the fridge produced no more cans and I had imbibed the last, last drop of the last, last Guinness leaving the hope that tomorrow I could refill the shelf. Hope is never lost.

"Ted, you should write for the company. They would sell out. Okay, it's time to see what the dinner looks like. I put it in the crockpot this morning before heading out to teach. My grandmother would put it in the oven all day long so that the meat was tender strings. It was probably dreadful, but as a kid I just loved it."

"Smells great," said Ted. He looked around the kitchen. "You know, it's funny, this place is totally different from the last one but everywhere you go, you make it yours."

"It helps to cart around a grand piano and all my wonderful paintings. And the best part about those paintings is that they're all done by relatives, friends, or people I've been privileged to meet. I'd rather have paintings than fancy appliances and furniture or a new car."

"You know what you're doing at the auctions. I love this old washstand, and the oak table is lovely."

I set the steaming plate of roast beef gravy, potatoes, carrots and parsnips in front of Ted, passed him the horseradish, and sat down with my own plate. "Bon appetite."

Ted delicately chewed a fork-full of beef and vegetables, and gave a moan of pleasure, "Just the way my mother used to make it. I love to taste the garlic and onions. Why on earth do they avoid those at retirement homes?"

"They don't all have your constitution, Ted. As a matter of fact, yours is better than mine. I can't handle horseradish."

We looked across the edge of the graveyard to the churning waters beyond. The setting sun gave the sky a pink hue, and as we enjoyed our food, we watched a freighter pass in one direction and a cruise ship in the other.

"It's late in the season for a cruise ship," said Ted.

"Maybe it was in for a refit after the season. Apparently, our ship builders are world-renowned. I know the ship I worked on, which was from the Netherlands, was refitted here. Some of the crew were telling me they got to hang out in Victoria for a couple of weeks while it was being done. They loved our city. They raved about different pubs like the Irish Times, and the Bard and Banker."

"Oh yes, I know the owner of those. He's a lovely chap."

"Me too. I played at one of his house parties. What an amazing job he did converting those beautiful old banks into memorable tourist places."

"My dear, you've had an interesting life with your career."

"I count my blessings every day. Now, Ted, how about a little more?"

"Yes, please." While I was getting him seconds, he said, with a laugh as he looked at the graveyard, "I've died and gone to heaven. And it's a handy place to do it in."

"What's been happening with you this week, Ted? Are you still having meetings about the store?"

"Oh sure, that seems to be an ongoing drama right now. I'd rather not discuss it. I've left it in the lawyer's hands."

"I guess that's a good idea. But still, I'm sure you want to understand the manager's position."

"Of course, I do. And I feel sick about what has happened. She and I have been friends for years, going way back to the Yukon. I certainly don't ever want to think badly of her. Such a bold, intelligent woman with a delightful wit. I wish she'd talked to me if she had problems. But I guess that's why the lawyers are removing me from it all. They know I'm emotionally involved and they just want to make things right."

"But you need honesty in any business you're associated with."

"Of course, you do," said Ted. "To change the subject, do you think we could go into the living room now? I've eaten far too much."

I put the dishes in the sink and the food away while Ted made his way into the next room. When I joined him, carrying two cups of tea, he said, "The highlight of my week was going to a school in Oak Bay – I forget the name of it but I've been there before. The Art teacher encourages the children to take chances. On this occasion, she got them reproducing my paintings, perhaps to prove the critics right." He glanced over at me to smile and then looked out the window again. "I can see why you moved here, Pet. It's a street with little traffic and the view is ever-changing. I must bring my scooter through the graveyard someday."

"Good idea, and don't forget to visit me while you're at it."

"Hopefully, you won't be lying in there before me. Now, where was I? Oh, yes, once the students have done their copies, she gets me to come in and talk to them about it. We have such a jolly time discussing how to create depth, size, colour, etcetera and they have so many very good questions."

"Like what?"

"For example, one young chap asked me if I'd ever seen igloos and polar bears. I told him that once I'd been out on a special boat that broke up the ice so that we could see that kind of thing in the Bering Sea. The man happened to be from Victoria, and he also took me out on a skidoo. And to think your current landlord was the driver."

"Yes, he asked me to remind you of that. The world is so small. Did you enjoy your time with him?"

"Not particularly. I hope he treats you well. He's a hard businessman."

"I'm sure it will be fine. You know, I'm so glad you do that sort of thing with school kids. I know what an influence you have on them. My students still talk about the little speech you gave to them before their piano recital. Your attitude about life affects kids at an important stage, and your encouragement means a lot."

"I hate to interrupt when you're singing my praises but look at the moon rising. Isn't it gorgeous?"

"Wow, it's huge. I thought it was only the harvest moons that were that big. You really need to put down your thoughts about the moon for posterity."

Ted didn't need encouragement. Within seconds, he was slowly speaking.

The Moon

The evening comes and the last of the fleecy clouds skirt across the sky, and in their wake, follows the golden orb of the moon. No matter what takes place on this earth, it shines serenely above all the carnage, all the wars, all the massacres and other distortions of humanity.

Of all the beings that look on the earth, the moon is the most serene. It sheds its light without requesting anything in return. Amidst the wildest orgies and struggles which attend humanity and the earth, it gives a message of calmness and tranquility. For centuries, it has acted as a beacon to lovers and those seeking a calmer view of life than the world possesses. It was here eons before mankind ever appeared and it will be here long after mankind has crucified itself with its ridiculous actions of greed and selfishness. Those intent on committing evil do not look at the moon because it would have a tranquilizing effect on their action. They are blind to its beauty and its message as it floats majestically above the earth, unchanging throughout the deprivations and the machinations bedeviling the world.

May the wild spirits of humanity emulate the moon and be like the princess in the castle – beautiful, calm and unattainable. Every night when the clouds have dispersed, the true glory of the moon shines out and we behold it with wonder. Long after we have disappeared, it will smile upon the world. Future generations will admire it when we are done and it will be there long after the generations are gone. May the moon's peace calm your troubled soul and may you float happily through life as she does.

"I like it, Ted," I said as I closed the notebook. "You're not just keeping it sweet and lovely. You're showing the yin and yang of life."

We sat contentedly watching the beautiful moon, without speaking. I mused that Ted was the only friend, or relative for that matter, that I could comfortably sit with, lost in thought. Actually, I reminded myself, I rarely even did this alone. I always had a book or a puzzle or journal that I was concentrating on, with music playing in the background.

Ted broke the silence saying, "Jan, I think it's time I got tucked into bed, if you don't mind driving me."

"Of course, Ted. Let me get your cane and coat. You've got a big staircase ahead of you."

I put on my coat and helped him with his. Using his cane, he got to the top of the rather steep steps and looked down. "Oh my, did I really climb these?"

"Do you think you can manage? The railing is secure and I've got you on this side."

Ted gripped the sturdy round rod. "Jesus, this metal is freezing."

Slowly, we made our way down. There wasn't a sound anywhere. Everyone must have been away for the weekend or something.

"Great work, Ted. We just have to walk to the gate now."

We were halfway there and suddenly Ted stopped.

"Ted, are you okay?" He seemed to have frozen. He was not responding. I held on tight and thought hard. I had heard that sometimes people with Parkinson's can freeze but I had never seen very much evidence of the Parkinson's with Ted, apart from a tremor in his hands. He had continued to paint despite this. He was getting heavy and it had been several decades since I was a nurse's aide. Should I lay him on the grass and run in and call someone? "Hello, is anyone there?" I tried shouting. It was dead quiet and there weren't even any cars going by on the street beyond the fence.

I looked at the moon and something made me start to sing softly. "*Blue Moon, you saw me standing alone, without a dream in my heart, without a love of my own.*"

91

Just then, Ted joined in singing. *"Blue Moon, you knew just what I was there for, you heard me saying a prayer for, someone I really could care for."* We continued to sing together, walking easily to the gate and then through it to the car.

Ted climbed into the small car with a sigh. I gratefully thought about the power of music and song as I got in, and started the cold engine.

"That was tiring, but I wouldn't have missed it for the world. Let's sing another song."

"Why don't you sing one of those rude army songs you used to sing for the ladies when you were at Carlton House?"

"They're not rude, you can take them two ways. You just have a dirty mind, my dear. Slightly raunchy is always acceptable."

He broke into song with perfect pitch, keeping me entertained as I drove him the few blocks to Sunrise. I knew the staff loved him and would make sure he was comfortable before he plunged into Dreamland.

Meeting the Boyfriend

"It's about time you two finally met," I said, concluding the introductions and watching Ted intently for his reaction. I could sense he wasn't too impressed. Artie and I had been seeing each other off and on for about three years. We seemed to be more off than on but we definitely had an amazing chemistry that kept pulling us together.

"Really nice to meet you, Ted," said Artie, sipping from a can of coke he had bought from the soft drink machine in the stairway on our way up. "I've got several older men I like to visit, that I worked with years ago. I like to see how they're handling the aging process. Everyone is different."

"Artie has asked me several times if he could join me, and today we were driving past on our way from town and we spontaneously came in. Hope you don't mind."

"No, that's good," said Ted in a monotone.

"Yes," said Artie. "She seems to always have an inspired time with you." He pointed to the small totem pole sitting on the floor beside the television. "There must be a good story behind that piece. Did a friend of yours do it?" asked Artie.

"Yes, as a matter of fact, he was a friend shortly after I talked him into joining my class," said Ted imperiously.

"So you have it here to remember that time?"

"The main reason I have it here is because I happen to appreciate art that is simple and meaningful."

"What is it you like about it?"

I glanced at Artie with a raised eyebrow. Was he goading him?

"I like the symbolism of the different creatures and I love the imagination that went into it. It reminds me of my time in the Yukon where I met several carvers. I actually do remember this carver's name. It was Stan Peters and he made it in the Yukon in the mid-70s, I believe. He is known in Whitehorse for the large totem he carved for the Rotary Peace Park."

Ted didn't make eye contact with Artie so Artie didn't respond. He simply swung his can with a relaxed wrist and waited. He was probably wondering why on earth I liked visiting this curmudgeonly man.

At last, Ted said, "Did you bring any chips with that coke? I'm dying for something crunchy and salty."

"You don't much like the food here then?" asked Artie.

"It's made for people without teeth or taste buds."

"Your nurse told me you couldn't have wasabi peas," I said. "But maybe you could have a few chips."

"To hell with the nurses," snapped Ted. "I don't want to be the healthiest one in the graveyard."

Artie laughed. "Hey, why don't you two enjoy your visit together? I feel like a third wheel. I'll go down to the pub for a beer and I'll bring back some chips."

"Maybe we could all go," I suggested.

"I don't want to go anywhere," interrupted Ted. "Please bring back those chips. That will be the best snack I could ask for."

"You've got it," said Artie. He rose to his full lanky height, shook Ted's hand, and kissed me suggestively on the lips. He gracefully avoided running into a table loaded with magazines, and ambled out the door.

"He's got a nice head of hair, I'll say that for him," said Ted. He stroked his moustache as he looked out the window.

"Okay, Mr. Harrison, what was all of that about?" I asked.

"All what?" asked Ted, innocently. He looked into my eyes with his honest face and I had to smile.

Trying to look stern, I said, "I know you don't suffer fools gladly, but Artie is no fool."

"Maybe not, but he's not as smart as you, or as generous, and you deserve better."

94

"How can you say that? He's gone to buy you what you asked for."

"He just wanted out of here and he knew I was on to him."

"Ted, you sound like a little kid. Are you jealous or something?"

"Maybe a little. But, Janet, why are you with a man like that? You told me yourself that he disappears for days. You can't trust him. He never takes you out. Just because he's good in bed is no—"

"*Ted,*" I interrupted,

"He's self-centred."

"Ted, I refuse to listen any more. It's time we wrote something down. Shall we hear about Potato Chips?"

"No, I'll speak about the snack I really wanted but knew he'd never find."

Wasabi Peas

I have a packet of wasabi peas: dry, green, crunchy and hot. As I munch the peas, visions of Japan come into my head. I see the moody islands and small boats flitting above the waves. Women in bright kimonos trip down to the beach and take their offspring for a paddle in the waves. With each crunchy bite of peas, I bring forth a further vision of Japan – all in a little packet. I do not need to pay the airfare or have a partner to enjoy the scene with me because all the little peas act as guides and lead my mind to things Japanese.

The very name Wasabi conjures up strange images of paintings by Hiroshige and such joy is contained in one little packet of wasabi peas.

"Oh, good. Now you're feeling better."

"No, I'm not – I'm starving. I need a snack."

I looked over his offerings. All he had were stale candies and cakes that various women had dropped off. "I put some cider in the fridge when we came in. Shall we split one even though it won't be too cold?"

"You angel, you. Let's each have one."

He took a sip and his eyes twinkled. I clinked my glass with his and joined him.

"That's better, Luv. I must apologize for my rudeness. I guess it was a bit of jealousy and a bit of worry. You need help picking out men."

"Artie is perfect for right now. Having a full-time man is a lot of work."

"It doesn't have to be. It should make your life easier and more enjoyable. Maybe I'm grumpy because I feel like I need a full-time woman in my life." After taking another sip, Ted said, "I am rather a good catch. It's a shame your student didn't think so. I certainly enjoyed our lunch together and she was quite beautiful for an older person. What did she say?"

"She said she would love to be your friend but she thought you were too old for her."

Ted laughed. "Weren't we the same age? Ah well," he said. "I probably *am* too old but it was fun to fantasize about that over lunch with her."

"If it's supposed to happen, it will happen, Ted." I started to laugh. "As if I know what I'm talking about."

"To hell with all this rubbish," said Ted, as he lifted his glass and looked at the bubbles. "We should write about cider."

Cider

Cider begins its life as an apple. A beautiful apple hangs on a tree and then it is picked and mixed with thousands of other apples, laughing and joking. Along comes the farmer and picks up these jolly apples and squeezes them in a press until their juice is emitted. All the jolly apples have turned into a laughing juice, which is then poured into a barrel and, still giggling, it is allowed to ferment. The giggling juice produces thousands of bubbles that bubble up to the surface and then the fermentation is stopped, and this precious golden liquid can be bottled and sealed.

All this distilled jollification is now purchased by the Cider lovers and can be extremely potent depending on how it is fermented. In fact, at one time, the British sailors of Portsmouth were forbidden to drink it because the result was so strong that they could scarcely walk up the gangplank. The name of this very strong cider is Scrumpy. It is not used for the delectation of modest ladies drinking in tearooms. It becomes the potent drink of roistering hooligans who can scarcely stagger out of the pub after drinking this distillation of Appledom.

Cider is the king of fruit juice blessed by the God of booze and it has come down through the years as one of the greatest products that apple producers can make. Long live cider – it helps to make harvesting merry and brings joy to the soul of apple lovers.

I put my book down and had a long drink. "Wonderful, Ted. As you know, this is one of my favourite drinks, so now, every time I have one, I'll be picturing giggling apples."

The nurse's aide came in, singing, "Hi, Ted, are you ready for bed?" quite loudly until she spotted me. "Oh, nice to see you again. You make Ted so happy."

"I'm not sure I did today but the cider is helping. How are you, Elena?"

"Bueno. I am good. I will come back later to get Ted to bed."

"Thanks so much. We won't keep him up much longer." I looked at my watch and wondered if Artie was planning on coming back any time soon. I didn't feel like having Ted say I told you so.

Ted stretched back in his easy chair and looked at the painting in front of him.

"Ted, I was wondering if you want me to change your paintings around in here. I think if I was looking at that one all the time, I'd get depressed." It was in dark colours and the subject was a table, with very inebriated men seated around it in a seedy pub. Today, it was depressing *me* as I thought about the many hours Art spent in a pub.

"Thank you for offering, and I might do that someday but this is by my friend, Norman Cornish. Do you know he worked in the mines for over thirty years? Most of his work shows the life of the average working person because that is what he was for so long."

"I can relate how nice it is to have art work around done by friends or at least people you've met. It makes the work all the more meaningful."

"Exactly. You know, I think I want to write a little about Life now."

"Sure, Ted," I said reaching for my book.

Ted closed his eyes and began to speak. Just then, Artie came in. I motioned for him to sit down.

Life Is Like the Weather

Yesterday was cloudy and my vision of the world, limited. I felt alone and devoid of friendship. But then, today, the sun broke through and friendship arrived. So, life takes on a more golden hue.

Life revolves around the weather of the mind. Luckily, there are no storms in sight, no shrieking winds, no deluges. The fresh breezes blow away the murky gossiping so that all my visions of friends remain unsullied by alien thoughts.

To retain a purity of thought and mind is indeed a problem. Peaceful acts can only be guaranteed by placid thoughts. Anything that unbalances the thought, unbalances the direction of the mind. Once the waters of the mind are placid, we must try to preserve that peaceful state.

We can only control our own minds and leave those of others to the gods they serve.

Ted opened his eyes and saw Artie sitting beside him. "Oh, hello, young man."

"Shall I open these for you, sir?" asked Artie, pointing to the big bag in his lap.

"Absolutely. I need something to go with this lovely cider."

"Oh, I'm glad you've been enjoying yourself." He put the opened bag in Ted's lap.

Ted took a handful and concentrated on crunching. At last, he smiled and said, "Arthur, I'm starting to like you." He drank the last of his glass.

Artie laughed and winked at me. "We men need a drink now and then to make the world right."

"We women do too," I said, polishing off my glass. I reached for some chips and between crunches asked Artie if he saw any of his buddies at the pub.

"Oh sure, the regulars are always there."

"Which pub do you like to go to?" asked Ted.

"I go to Bartholomew's. They have live music most nights, although I don't usually last for more than one set. I can't seem to stay up the way I used to."

"Will you take me there sometime?" asked Ted.

"Sure, it will be noisy but you can always take your hearing aids out. That's what my mother does when I take her there."

"How old is your mother?"

"She's eighty-two going on eighteen. She lives in Manitoba but she goes travelling all the time. Have you heard of the red hats? There will be a busload of them and they're all wearing a red hat. She loves to party. I guess that's where I get it from."

"Well, next time she's in town, let's all go out. I would enjoy that."

"You're asking for it, Ted. I'm sure that can be arranged," said Artie.

Ted crunched a few more chips and seemed totally relaxed and happy.

I stood up and gave Ted a kiss. "We're heading home, Ted, but thanks so much for having us. Next time let's go out on the town."

"Good idea. I want dinner and music. And, Artie, if you don't mind, I want Jan all to myself."

"I understand, Ted. Of course. She's a great gal."

We walked out and I realized I was feeling much happier than when I came in. Was it the cider or was it that Ted had somewhat accepted Artie?

Another Strange Night Out

"Where are we going for dinner again?" asked Ted as I scanned the road for a close parking spot.

"It's called Superior, because it's on Superior St, but not necessarily for its quality."

"Shouldn't we be aiming for quality?"

"The parking angel is with us again," I announced, as I eased into a small spot out front.

Pulling the walker from my trunk, I brought it around for Ted to use on his own. He hoisted himself from the car and as we walked, I said. "When I saw the unusual décor in this place, I knew you had to see it."

"I believe this used to be the Unitarian church. I went here now and then." We slowly made our way up the sidewalk to the entrance of the brick building, with Ted manoeuvring his walker from one side to the other. He wasn't inclined to go in a straight line, which was perhaps symbolic of his life.

"I like the musicians that are playing tonight," I said. "Ben is a soulful clarinet player and Larry has backed him on guitar for decades. They're good buddies."

While we waited to be seated, Ted gazed around the large room. "The owner must be a taxidermist," he said. There were deer heads on the wall, and stuffed crows on overturned chairs placed on a small balcony that ran around the top of the room. It probably was once where the choir would have stood. We waited beside a painting of a skeleton dancing on a hill that was shimmering with autumn colours.

"What do you think of his technique, Ted?" I asked.

"The colours are beautiful," said Ted. "Rather strange subject matter though."

"The father of the owner is a painter and he has a gallery on the floor below. Maybe we should visit him after dinner."

We were taken to a table at the back of the room, which made it perfect for watching people, hearing the music and being able to converse. Ted stared through the glass of the table top to the display of bird and rodent remains, including talons, bones and feathers. Ted laughed. "It's very creative but certainly it's weird. Will it put you off your meal?"

"Ted, I've been known to be the only one chowing down in the dining room of a heaving ship. It would seem nothing puts me off food, especially if I don't have to cook," I said.

Ted looked across at a painting of a naked man. "He's not even beautiful. I might have to ask them to drape that one."

"My aunt did that to a large nude painting I used to have when she visited me once. I kept the scarf around her long after Margie went home because it reminded me of her. She was such a sweetheart."

The waiter came over dressed in a black tee shirt and kilt. "I'd like a glass of Merlot, please," I said.

"And you, sir?"

"Sure, I'll have one of those too."

Ted was studying the menu. "It seems they only have appetizers that cost as much as an entrée. I hope they're a decent size. I can't imagine halibut cheeks being large."

"They're called tapas, Ted. That seems to be the trend now – where you get small plates and share. It's lucky neither one of us tend to eat a lot at one time. Does anything appeal?"

"Curried scallops with radishes. What a combination. But let's try them. What tickles your fancy?"

"Jerk chicken with yam pakora."

"Okay, and let's add the cheese and fig plate," said Ted.

The waiter brought our wine and took our order. "Is the chicken tender?" I asked.

"Oh, indeed," he assured me. "It will melt in your mouth."

Soon, we had settled in with our wine, and were listening to Ben and Larry play a slow version of *In a Mellow Tone*.

"Thank you for this experience, my dear. It *is* an experience," he said, observing a cat that was sleeping on a window ledge. "I think that cat is *not* stuffed."

We clinked our glasses and I giggled when they started to play *Old Folks*. We happily observed our neighbours and listened to a couple of more tunes without talking.

The musicians took a break and came over to say hello. Ben set his beer down to shake Ted's hand.

"Do you find you play music better if you have a drink?" asked Ted.

"Well, I think I do but probably I'm the only one that thinks so," laughed Ben.

Larry came and stood beside him, and heard Ted ask if he needed to worry now about drinking and driving with the new, stricter laws.

Larry laughed. "Jan, hasn't he ever offered you peanut butter after a gig?"

I smiled. "The old peanut butter trick."

Ben had a long drink from his beer and rubbed the froth from his moustache. Still standing, he gestured with enthusiasm as he said, "I've escaped more roadblock checks with my peanut butter ploy. It covers alcohol beautifully. Not that I drink all that much nowadays. After all, I'm seventy-four. But I have some good memories."

Our meals arrived so the two wandered off after wishing us a fun evening.

Three lonely scallops swam in an oily yellow pool on a long, thin plate with chopped radishes providing a colourful patch. The other plate had two skewers of chicken with 3 small pieces on each and there was a small, deep fried pakora. Ted chuckled as he watched me divvy up our small meal. "I'm so glad we're getting one and a half scallops. Don't give me the big half, as I couldn't do it justice."

Ted placed a bite of chicken in his mouth, and chewed and chewed. I watched him and started to giggle. "I can see it's melting in your mouth." Ted rolled his eyes and kept chewing.

The musicians came back to the stand and began playing *The Shadow of your Smile*.

We had soon polished off our meal. "The flavours were delicious, I'll give them that," I said. "And we've still got our cheese plate, I nearly forgot," I said as the waiter placed the tiny plate between us and took away the other dishes.

The waiter offered us another glass of wine and I agreed but Ted went for coffee. The atmosphere was too enjoyable to rush, even though there were more people waiting to be seated.

I spread some gorgonzola cheese on a cracker and handed it to Ted. He ate delicately, while I rummaged in my purse for some lipstick.

"Did you bring some writing paper?" asked Ted.

"I must have something. Are you feeling inspired?"

He had a sip of coffee and then began to speak.

Music

As Shakespeare said, 'the isle is full of noises, sounds, and sweet airs which give delight and hurt naught. Sometimes a thousand twangling instruments will hum about mine ears and sometimes voices, that when I woke, I cried to dream again.'

Music transports us to the imaginative world of perfection. It transcends the bounds of ordinary existence and leads us into a happy or contemplative frame of mind. The cacophony of modern music does nothing for the soul but lets us be loud and free in a way that buries feeling and contemplation. Great music, on the other hand, lifts us to paradise more than any other art.

Beethoven stirs the soul and takes us straight to heaven so instead of staying moribund on the earth, we raise to greater visions and feelings, which merge on perfection. On the other hand, jazz is complete freedom from formalism, where the musician is able to add their personality and character to the music. So, it is unique in human qualities, especially those that are of a revolutionary nature.

Music can be crazy, personal and infinitely wonderful. Without music, the world would be a much duller place and humanity would be all the poorer for it. Let us, therefore, dance and sing with the delight that it brings. It is said that music hath charms and so it has. Long live music!

I put my pen and paper aside and spread some cheese and fig on a cracker for each of us.

"Ted, how can you quote from Shakespeare so easily? You are so good with the English language; it must help to have such a good memory. I wish I were better with words. But guess what?"

"I can't imagine," said Ted, his fingers clasped across his belly and his face glowing like Buddha's.

"I've found a wonderful woman friend, who is a published writer, and she has been looking over some of my songs and tweaking the words, and just one word changed can make such a difference. I don't know if we'll do anything with them – she's also a lovely singer – but I love the fun of working on something creatively with someone else."

"Of course, that can really enhance the creative process," agreed Ted. "As long as people don't have an agenda around the fate of it, I believe the writing fairies will assist."

"Do you really believe that?"

"Sure, the best creations come from stepping aside from your own personality and letting something else come through. You multiply that by two when you have a friend working with you. That's what you and I are doing."

"Maybe you could speak in rhymes so that I could put some music to it? Shall we try right now?"

The waiter refilled Ted's cup and I had another sip of wine.

Rhyme One

I see before my jaded eyes, a vision bursting from the skies,

With hair, so blonde and beautiful, it fills my thoughts with dreams so cool.

This angel for me it will suffice, I need not go to paradise.

She smiles and then my heart feels free. A noble girl just meant for me.

Her voice and breath are like the breeze, which flutters through the dainty trees.

And there when verdant blossoms grow, her lively mind begins a flow

Of ecstasy, which lights my life and chases off the thoughts of strife.

"Amazing, Ted. There aren't too many people that can rhyme like that off the top of their head. And thank you for the compliments. I don't think I'll put that to music but I'll treasure it."

"Oh, I forgot about putting it to music. I think having music in the background is making this easier than it should be. I do like your friends. I love the atmosphere they create."

"I don't know them very well; we've never associated with each other outside of music but you know the music community in Victoria is full of wonderful people. I'm so grateful to be a part of it."

"The reason artists are so interesting, in my opinion, is that they have spent hours perfecting their crafts. It requires being alone and away from a routine, and other people's opinions. Let's have one last try at a poem and then you should take me back, if you don't mind."

"Of course," I said, poising my pen over the paper.

Rhyme Two

My love is a bird flying so free, but alas, I can't see the branch of a tree.

And so, I just fly into the air, and finally am filled with a deep, sad despair.

And so, love is lost for wandering alone, with no place to settle and call it a home.

I once loved freedom and found to my cost that when love is free, it often gets lost.

But that doesn't stop me from soaring so high that I lose all the sight of the one who'd be nigh.

A bird is so happy when flying so free and yet, to find rest it needs a fine tree.

But alas, I've been soaring so very high, that I can't find a tree from up in the sky.

And then when I wish to finally land, I find it's a desert all covered in sand.

There are only large sand dunes, no trace of a branch, to finally settle but luckily per chance,

My love finds the same spot where I have flown and shares then with me, the love that I own.

The waiter came over to collect our payment and we prepared to leave.

"I can't say I'm satisfied with a full belly but I certainly feel satisfied," said Ted. "Are there any other places to dine that have live music?"

"Artie's Mom is coming out from Manitoba next month. Let's go to the pub and hear some loud dance music," I suggested. "I love watching people that know how to dance."

"Do you dance?" asked Ted.

"Musicians rarely bother to learn how to dance. I've got rhythm but I've never learned the steps so I step on dancers' feet. I figure when I retire, I'll learn to dance."

"You'll never retire."

"You're probably right, Ted." We stood outside, Ted leaning on his walker and gazing around at the peaceful evening. There were very few cars, and the streetlights revealed blossoms and fresh new leaves.

"Spring is my favourite time of year," said Ted. We ambled slowly to the car, grateful for another special evening together.

Pub Joys

It's too loud in here," said Ted, swivelling his head from side to side to survey the boisterous pub. No one else seemed to mind that the musicians were playing at top volume.

"Take your hearing aids out, Ted," I said. "Here, give them to me." As I put them in a pocket of my purse, I pulled out my own musician earplugs with filters that I always kept handy.

Once both of us had comfortable ears, we grinned at each other. "I love it here," shouted Ted. "And the music is good."

It was Sunday night and a band I used to play with were doing an early gig that only went until 10:00, so I knew I could still get Ted back before curfew.

Ted clinked his chocolaty Guinness with my cider. When we came in, we had walked past the table Artie was sharing with three other men. He offered to get us chairs, but I pointed to a table at the back of the room, away from the speakers. It wasn't much better. Randy Tucker liked to play loud, but he was a wonderful singer/guitarist that performed an array of genres. I knew Ted would recognize most of the tunes. He was singing, "*It's a little bit funny, this feeling inside …*" I hummed along with the James Taylor song as I watched Artie say something to his bachelor buddies. Knowing him, he was asking questions to redirect the conversation to something he was interested in. Like me, he was a Gemini who got bored easily.

Ted's foamy moustache dribbled when he asked me if I knew the band. I nodded.

"Can we order some chips?"

"You mean French fries," I shouted.

"Nothing French about them."

The band announced a break and I handed Ted his hearing aids. Artie came over to join us.

"I thought you were bringing your mother to meet me," said Ted.

"She had to change her flight to next week. One of her friends died."

"One by one we lose our friends," said Ted. "Did your mother have a career?"

"She was a nurse that worked her way up to being the head nurse at the hospital she worked at in Manitoba. They called them Matrons back then in the nursing community."

"And she was a wife and mother? What was her name?"

"Dorothy had four kids."

"She must be a wonder woman."

"She's a dynamo. After my dad died, she really started to enjoy herself. She loves to travel. To tell you the truth, Ted, I don't think she's at all interested in a relationship. She really appreciates her independence. But I'm sure she'd like to meet you."

"Jan's mother has the same name but I suspect I'd enjoy your mother more. She sounds like fun."

"She was sure different than my friends' mothers. I'm going on a road trip with her in Saskatchewan in the fall. She's pretty cool to hang out with."

Randy came over and gave me a hug. I introduced him to Ted and Ted told him how much he liked his music. "Do you know any country music?"

"A little," said Randy.

"He knows lots," I said. "He worked with Ian Tyson for years."

"My favourite is Frank Sinatra and I love the way Jan backs me up. Will you play a couple of tunes with us?"

"Sure, I'd love to," I said.

"We'll call you up in the next set."

"So, Artie, how do you earn your money?" asked Ted.

Art laughed. "What money? I'm afraid I've never been very interested in working a normal job. And I'm also not good at investing money. Right now, I own a luxury van and I take groups of people on day tours from the cruise ships. I take them to see the sights – you know, the castle, Chinatown, old buildings and out to Butchart Gardens. I'm interested in history so I enjoy sharing what I appreciate about this place."

"You must be a bit of an actor then," said Ted.

"I wish I were," said Artie. "I can't fake it when people are annoying."

Ted laughed and said, "I seem to have a similar problem."

The music started up and Randy sang Desperado. Ted handed me his hearing aids again. The band segued into Sway and people were soon crowding the dance floor. Randy introduced me, and I waved to the bass player and drummer before trading seats with Kal, the keyboardist, who seemed to be glad of the break. Sounding like Sinatra, Randy crooned *Witchcraft*. I felt energized to be playing with my old friends, and also to have Ted sitting, smiling and tapping his fingers on the table. I grinned as he turned to look at the table beside him where a very drunk woman was speaking heatedly while her partner stroked her arm with long sensuous strokes. Ted's gaze fell on the bar and soon the waitress was leaning over him, her ample bosom falling from her low-cut t-shirt.

Randy slowed the feel and started singing *You Make Me Feel So Young*. He signalled me to take a solo and watched from under the brim of his hat, his smirk of pleasure goading me to show off. We ended it with the cartoon ending we had come up with years ago.

I came back to the table to find Ted with a mouth full of French fries. "Have a chippy, my dear."

As I nibbled on some fries, Ted said, "I so enjoyed watching you. So bouncy, bouncy and fitting right in with the rest of them. Oh, and that's an Elvis song."

Artie came over and pulled me out of my seat. "Dance with me."

I saluted to Ted and moved into Artie's arms. Although we had never had lessons, we were pretty smooth. We had met on a dance floor a few blocks away three years before.

Art whispered in my ear, "People know from the way we move, how amazing our sex life is."

I stared into his big brown eyes and responded to his kiss.

Artie went back to his table and I suggested to Ted that we go across the hall to the Oyster Bar where the music wasn't so overpowering.

We settled the bill and the waitress kindly said she'd bring our drinks to the other bar. Ted gamely leaned on his cane as we followed her. Plopping into a booth with leather seats, we both let out a sigh of relief. The band was now just pleasant background music.

"Let's order oysters," said Ted.

"You're hungry tonight."

"Not really. I just like food I never get at Sunrise."

"I like food I don't have to cook."

We placed our order with a jovial waitress.

"I think I've been here before," said Ted, gazing around at the prints of fox hunts on the walls. "Let's write a poem, Jan. I've got an idea."

Scrambling for my journal, I barely caught up to Ted's slow, resonant voice.

The World Is My Oyster

Oysters are a rare food, which grow slowly inside a shell, and when we take the shell from the oyster, it's known as shucking. Shucking is the art of breaking the shell and forcing the live oyster to be exposed and then eaten. So, we can look upon the world as our oyster – but to enjoy it fully, we have got to break the shell and taste the live oyster inside. The world is an adventure only if we break the shell to sample the contents. Not everyone enjoys eating oysters but those who develop a taste for them find that they are absolutely rewarding. They titillate the taste buds and open the joys of the oyster to the person who wishes to experience the pleasure rendered to the taste buds.

We must sample as many of the oyster joys of the world as we can in order to find gratification for our various taste buds. There are many ways to find the oysters of life. For some, music provides the thrill of a new experience. For others, literature and books provide another type of thrill. And yet, for a third group, landscape and the joy of seeing nature in all its wonders can be extremely satisfying. In other words, life is full of varied 'oysters' that help to enlarge the experience of living and finding new joys, which can be unexpected. Lucky is the person who comes across a new joy in life, which they had not formerly foreseen.

Before moving to my little room, I had known of course, that birds fly. But being on the fourth floor of a large apartment house can be above the height at which many birds fly and in consequence, I have found a new oyster opened which is – bird flight. When one is at ground level, it's hard to walk with your head looking up at the sky all the time. When I am on the fourth floor, I look down into a wooded valley in which the main types of birds, namely crows and gulls, disport themselves.

On close observation, I have come to the conclusion that birds get quite a lot of fun and enjoyment in skimming between the trees and above them. The observer can then share in the joys of flight while remaining attached to the earth. Crows appear to lack a grace in flight, which belongs to the gulls. The crow family seems to labour in flight whereas the gulls appear to enjoy gliding and flying in small groups to various tall buildings and trees. The gulls take advantage of the breezes through which their bodies glide while the crows work to achieve height and do not cruise so effortlessly through the air.

Probably from the human point of view, the art of flying is nature's gift of an oyster to the birds, especially when it appears so natural and unforced. As the humans form their own happy experiences in life, so do the birds. We must watch them carefully and study their aerobatics in order to enjoy the business of flying. This requires imagination so that humans can endeavour to sample what it is that brings such joy to the flying birds.

There are species of animals that give birth to their young, and then enjoy the power of flight in their hunting and general behaviour. We do not know how mammals feel when flying but we can surmise that the world is their oyster.

I noticed that Ted brought the poem to an end rather abruptly. It was probably because the oysters had arrived and he couldn't resist them. Immediately, he scooped up a shell and sucked the meat into his mouth.

"Glorious, my dear. Do dig in."

"Are they alive?" I asked.

"No, more's the pity. But they haven't overcooked them. I love the texture."

I tentatively reached for a shell, put it on my side plate, and used a knife and fork to take a small bite. "Sometimes my tummy doesn't like shell-fish so I'm a bit nervous." I chewed daintily then suddenly I felt ravenous. Without speaking, we cleaned the plate up in record time. The waitress laughed when she took the plate away. "Would you like another order?"

Ted started to nod but I said, "No, we have to leave pretty soon. Just the bill is great."

"Good decision, Jan. I would have eaten those all night. When was the last time you had oysters?"

"I'm not sure it was the last time, but I was remembering following a creek down to the ocean on Quadra Island one summer with my partner, and we found an oyster bed and wonderful tide pools to swim in. We took a load of oysters back to our cabin and had a little fire outside with a simple grate over it and put the oysters on top, and they were so fresh and delicious. All they needed was butter, salt and pepper."

"You were eating outside too, which makes it all the more special."

"That is so true, Ted. I think that's why I love picnics so much. It's so nice to share the elements in the elements. But speaking of elements, there's a wind warning tonight so maybe we should think about heading home."

The waitress came over with the bill. Ted said to her, "We'd like some tea and I'd love to see the dessert list."

I chuckled. "Ted, you're having too much fun."

"I hope you don't mind, Jan, but I think I might have another poem to spout off."

"Not at all, Ted, and I can always drink tea."

When the waitress returned with two pots of Earl Grey, Ted looked up from the menu and said, "Is the apple pie fresh?"

"Of course, sir, this is a high-class joint."

Ted laughed. "Excellent. One large piece with ice cream and cheese, and two forks."

Settling back in his seat, Ted waited for me to find my pen and he was off.

The Wind

The wind, the wind, the wind, has many human characteristics. It can be light and tender, and it can blend with the sun as a sweet flowing breeze. Rarely does it get angry. But when its temper gets rough, it snaps whole trees in half and litters the forest with broken branches. Otherwise, it can be gentle and just have enough force to blow dying flower petals, coating the ground with their colours.

One fall day, I was driving from Edmonton to the Yukon in my car. It was a sunny autumn day with a light wind. The golden leaves had fallen onto the road and created a carpet that was about six inches deep. As I raced the car through them, it seemed like real gold was rising up around me. This was one of nature's magic tricks where nature made the golden road fly into the air. Such moments can't be planned. I was lucky to be there at that time to witness the leaves and trees working together to create a magic effect.

Even when dead, the leaves have a strange new life. They brighten up the roadway and the path and they flutter like birds before settling down. A few days later, the rain comes and the leaves lie heavy, and they slowly fertilize the gardens and field with their dead bodies.

The wind is at its cruelest when winter arrives because the breezes no longer refresh. Nature hibernates until the spring when the sun brings its own magic to the world, and the trees bear more new leaves and a new life is given to everything.

The winds of spring are gentle breezes and serve to move the new life and its fresh green robes. This new life has risen from the ashes of its ancestors.

There's nothing more refreshing than a cool wind on a summer's day. We can inhale its goodness and enjoy the refreshing movement of its breath. The air ceases to be stale, and the oxygen it contains is blown hither and thither through the countryside so that one really appreciates the liveliness of the air over vast distances. For years, it was a source of real power in the world and ships would set their sails to explore this movement. For centuries, ships could only move with the labour of their oarsmen or with the wind filling their canvas.

We owe a lot to the history of the wind. It has given us power for many generations. Now we don't even need it as the source of power but it's getting stronger than ever. Perhaps, this is the time to take full advantage of it.

"At least we have windmills that people use now, although there seems to be controversy about them," I said as I laid my journal aside. I put milk in my tea and smiled as I watched Ted dive into the pie.

He swallowed a large piece and said, "Bloody hell, this is good. Why on earth can't we have pie at Sunrise?"

"Well, Ted, you *are* diabetic," I said, angling my fork in to scoop up some covered in ice cream. "You're right – it's fantastic. Maybe I should protect your health and eat the rest of it."

"No bloody way," laughed Ted, pushing my fork out of the way.

I watched Ted motor through the pie, as I listened to the music. I thought about Artie in the next room and how I was so much more comfortable here with Ted. Gratitude filled my heart as I realized that even though Ted and I had a limited relationship, he was a man that I could relax and be myself

114

with. Artie was a challenge at the best of times. Maybe I should be glad he spent so little time with me.

As if he could read my thoughts, Ted said, "I think I've figured out why you spend time with Artie, even though he's never going to be the guy you'll settle down with."

"Ted, I've tried settling. It wasn't very satisfying. I was lonely. At least in this relationship, I'm free to hang out with my friends whenever I like. But what's your theory?"

"He's the first guy you've really let yourself go with. I can tell you have exciting sex. But someday you'll experience a deep and meaningful relationship, with someone you never get bored with, who will treat you with the adoration you deserve."

"Is that what you had, Ted?"

Ted didn't immediately reply. He looked away, as if in deep thought. Then he said, "On rare occasions, I have seen the relationships I'm referring to. They are worth waiting for, I'm sure."

"You're probably right, Ted. Is it fear that holds me in dysfunctional relationships? When I grow up, I'm not going to be afraid of anything."

"Fear is a waste of time," said Ted. "Let's do a quick poem about that."

Fear

Life goes happily along until there comes catastrophe. We are sailing on an untroubled sea. Suddenly, the wind whips up the waves and they become much larger. Our pleasant barque is lifted and then dropped to the frenzy of the waters. Finally, we realize that we cannot control our surroundings. Panic displaces calm and fear displaces joy.

What we cannot control, we fear and what has appeared to be a nursery rhyme existence becomes a tale of terror. The sky mirrors our feelings. Storm clouds and winds disturb the quiet tenor of life, and we are borne willy-nilly to goals we have not envisaged. The mild panic and fear give way to horrific moods which we have never experienced before.

Physically, we are helpless, and beads of sweat drip from our tortured faces and bodies. We tremble uncontrollably and hope dissipates. We are lost in a strange world – frightening in its intensity. Prayers and supplications are in vain, for the forces of nature do not listen to the cries of humanity. Even those with faith are destroyed by the calamity, which engulfs everyone. Deep fear – deeper than the greatest ocean – engulfs us and we are swept away to infinity, tortured and screaming. There is no God to hear us and no spirit of divine intervention to save us. We depend on humanity, and humanity is forsaken and lost. Fear and terror have enveloped us. All is catastrophe.

I put the journal in my purse and said, "That about sums up how ridiculous fear is. Are you saying that most of it is in our imagination?"

"Not at all," said Ted. "Fear is a very important part of the human condition. But it's not necessary to make it such a big part of our psyche. We shouldn't let it take hold unless it's absolutely necessary."

"Like if a bear is chasing us?"

"As we age, we look back and see how fear held us back from being the best we could be in this short life. I see you as moving forward despite your fears. That takes courage."

"Thank you, Ted. I wish I were as fearless as you. But you might be quaking in your boots when the Matron at Sunrise gives you hell. Let's settle up and get out of here."

"My dear, this has been a splendid night," said Ted as we bundled ourselves into our coats.

Renos and Dreams

I was humming *When I Fall in Love* as I parked the car in front of Sunrise, and realized that I was happy. It had been a difficult and lonely spring and summer for me since Artie and I had ended our relationship. I sorely missed our beautiful intimacy, but we both knew we didn't have enough in common for the long term. How strange to have amazing chemistry and love each other but have opposite goals and needs. Ah well, we'd given it a good try and I had so many things going on, I didn't have time to tackle the dating game. The latest thing I'd done was buy a one-bedroom condo in an old building, and was looking forward to renovating and updating it.

I ran up the back stairs to Ted's room, determined to get him out into this glorious sunny day. As I came out from the stairwell, I passed a room where they had a large movie screen for the residents. There was Ted, in his wheelchair, all by himself, watching a show. I sat down beside him.

"I'm so glad you're here, Dear. Watch the end of this show with me. It's so interesting."

We held hands and watched incredible photography of planets and stars hurtling through space. It was a documentary on the world as we know it, coming to an end.

When it was over, he said, "You know, I often have dreams like that. Maybe it really will happen."

"You *do* seem to have an interest in what's beyond the earth. I'm not very well informed when it comes to world events, so you probably have more insight than me, Ted. What do you think are the odds that we might have a disaster and disappear?"

"It's not worth losing sleep over but from that documentary's perspective we certainly look very fragile."

"I just know we have to enjoy every minute of the Now. Which is why I'm here. To take you outside. Why are you in your wheelchair? You're so close to your room, you could use your walker."

"I had a fall today. Let's go back to my room. The girl said she'd be back to take me but I'd much rather have you do it."

"Of course, Ted, but are you hurt? What happened?"

As I pushed him, he explained. "I don't quite know how it happened. Maybe I have too much in my room so I tripped on something. I found myself on the floor and the girls got me sorted out quite quickly."

Ted relaxed into his big, comfy chair in his room and I checked him out. "You do have a little cut and bruising here on your head. Do you feel okay?"

"Sure, no problem."

"Would you like me to push you through Beacon Hill Park? Maybe there will be another ball game to watch, or a concert. The fresh air would be good for you."

"I'm feeling very lazy so let's just visit here. Now tell me, when do you get your condo?"

"Next week I get the key and the same day a demolition crew is taking out a wall. Then we start renovations, which I hope will be done in a month so I can move in. No more renting finally, and a new bathroom and a kitchen with a view!"

"I thought you were buying a little house?"

"The mortgage would have been too much pressure. Besides, I've never lived in a multiple unit building. It will be fun to have a bit of a community."

"You'll enjoy it, as long as you can play the piano and entertain."

"I think concrete buildings are pretty soundproof. Well, Ted, if we're not going out, maybe we better write something down."

"Yes, I can't stop seeing those pictures in that TV show in my mind."

He stared out the window at the sky as I found something to write on.

Time

A few billion years ago, where I'm sitting was flaming gas. The world had just been born and really was far too hot to even consider visiting. Then, along came time, slow and inexorable.

Things gradually cooled down like Tam o' Shanter's wife, and then the little creatures that were microscopic in size developed and started eating one another. This led to them becoming bigger and soon the world was full of creatures of all sizes eating one another. Naturally, their numbers increased, owing to the magic of sex.

Finally, mankind emerged and then indiscipline entered the world. Greedy, greedy mankind took what it wanted and flourished until the whole place was given over to the needs of humans.

I am now sitting in the same spot as the boiling gas but it is so tame and quiet that I cannot compare it to the past. However, time brings its own surprises and tomorrow we could be enveloped in flames as of yore.

Let us give time its due. It can bring havoc and tragedy but also absolute peace and tranquility. I wish to fade out in a tranquil period but time will go on forever.

"I'm glad we don't worry about a calamity happening," I said. "Your motto seems to be, 'relax without fear.'"

Ted laughed. "Perhaps, it's all an illusion. Actually, I think there's a lot going on behind the scenes that very few know about, but since we can't do anything about fearful people with power, we need to pretend everything is happening as it should."

I wondered if I should bring up one of my beliefs that most of my friends thought was airy fairy. "Ted, do you think there's any value in large groups of people meditating on things like world peace, respect for the planet, ending of poverty, etcetera. I think that's how most churches developed. They could see how much stronger prayer became when more than one person was tuning into a higher power – even if that higher power is within."

"Yes, of course, we can change frequencies of other dimensions. Even though we can't see something, doesn't mean it isn't real. Just like the Reiki you do on me. I feel a shift that can't be explained by Science but there are millions of people that benefit from Touch Therapy."

"Ted, I love that you're so open-minded."

Just then, the door opened and a young woman asked Ted if he needed anything.

"Yes, Dear, I would like you to ask them to bring me a tray for dinner. I don't want to go downstairs today and I'm going to have an early night."

"I'm sure they can make an exception for you, Ted, since you had a fall today. You look like you're feeling better," she said. "Enjoy your visit."

She closed the door behind her and Ted said, "I forgot I had a fall today. Maybe we should write something about that if you're willing?"

"Love to, Ted."

Feet

Feet are useful when you think of all the weight we balance on two feet and how everyone's feet are quite small to hold up the size of the body. My feet are particularly small. It's like balancing on a pinhead – but they do their job and rarely complain. I've had them for eighty-five years and they've never let me down yet. However, I still need a wheeler when I go out, to make sure my legs are steady. Otherwise, I'm walking on my head.

I've had three falls and each one is an experience. I've fallen twice on the back of my head and once on the front of my head but they didn't seem to do a lot of damage, so there must be a brain in there. To lose one's balance can be a sign of old age and I am not ashamed to be showing a few signs of old age. Sometimes my memory goes – Ploop! It drops into a pool of something and I have to think hard to remember where I am.

My friend, Barry, phones every night and asks me what I've done in a day and I can't always remember – largely due to the fact that I haven't done much. But I always remember when my friend, Jan, comes. The golden-haired vision comes after she has been teaching the piano, and she teaches me what grace, beauty and intelligence are all about. The night is dark but when she appears, it lights up like a big lamp in the night, and I go to bed with pleasant thoughts and dreams. So, her visits are very important for my peace of mind.

I sit alone for most of my day in my little turret on top of Sunrise Castle, and see the birds disporting themselves in the air and the trees waving in the breeze, and there are lots of interesting things to see.

But best of all, I like preparing for bed and when I take my socks off, I see those dainty toes waving in the air. They won't get covered up until tomorrow morning so they can continue to wiggle all night long. The nervous system is amazing. The top of your body can tell your toes to move. At least somebody does your bidding and my toes are faithful servants.

"Why don't you take your shoes off right now, Ted," I suggested as I put the paper aside. "I'll give your feet a massage and you can fall asleep if you want."

Ted pushed himself into a prone position in the chair and moaned with pleasure. "If I were a cat, I'd be purring right now."

As I worked on Ted's feet, I observed how tiny they were for his size and how amazingly youthful his skin was. When I was finished with his feet, I went behind him to do a little Reiki on his head. Ted was a fun person to practise on because he was so appreciative and trusting. He seemed to be sleeping, although he was very quiet about it. Didn't older people usually snore?

I decided I would leave him and go for a walk on my own through Beacon Hill Park before I went home to continue my many renovation plans. Picking out colours, tiles, lighting, sinks, flooring and appliances was my latest delight in life. I tried not to dwell on the fact that it was strange to do it alone. It was easy to think there was something wrong with me if I went down that road.

As I was putting on my sweater, Ted opened his eyes. "Oh Jan, thank you so much. You put me in a beautiful dream state. I'm sure you want to get outside but I was thinking, maybe we should write something short about dreams."

"Of course, I'm jealous that I rarely remember mine."

Dreams

I close my eyes against the sunlight streaming into the room. Then, I drift away from this place to an alien land, which is magnificent in its colour and form.

Resplendent mountains lie on the horizon like golden thrones in the sunlight. Each dream brings a new vision. Last week, I visited Japan and walked under the Torii, which was a bright red. People wore gowns of vivid hue and the sun shone with a pink light casting a lively glow over the whole dream world. I have seen India in my dreams, and gazed upon waving palms heavy with coconut and bright white beaches baking under hot suns.

Then, I hear a noise. My doorbell rings and I return to cold reality. The dreams must wait for another time but they will return, I know. Alas, no one can share them with me. I am quite alone in the dreams and can only describe what I remember of the whole mosaic.

What a pleasure it is to visit another world so frequently. Perhaps, tomorrow another great vision awaits and once again, I shall dwell in the unseen lands of dreams and all without drugs.

"Ted, that was beautiful. Were you dreaming about Japan just now?"

"No, it was more to do with what I was watching in the movie room. But we had already written something about that, hadn't we?"

"That's right. Okay, Ted, it's time for me to get some exercise. I've got a little gig tonight at Ocean Point with a trio so I won't be getting much there apart from loading my keyboard into the hotel."

"Don't they have a piano?"

"Very few do these days, Ted. Ah well – it's all good. I love playing with sax and bass. I'll see you in a few days."

"I'm going back to Dreamland," said Ted as he squirmed deeper into the chair. I put a blanket over his bare toes and let myself out.

Vietnam Garden Restaurant

"You *did* make a reservation, didn't you, Ted?"

"No. We don't need a reservation with Ken."

"But it's Valentine's Day, and it's a popular place."

Ted smiled and shrugged. I pulled up at the loading zone by the front door and told Ted I would be right back. The place was packed and I could see Ken behind the counter quickly stirring and flipping things on the stove. However, when he looked up to see who was coming in, his face broke into a grin.

"Is Ted with you?" he asked, not missing a beat as he passed the spatula over to his assistant. He followed me outside as Shelly, his wife, rushed to make a table available near the kitchen. Opening the passenger door, he flowed with good cheer as he helped Ted get out of the car. Leaning on Ken and his cane, Ted made his way inside with shouts of laughter as I got in the car to move it to the rear parking lot.

When I returned, Ted was settled at a makeshift kitchen table squeezed into a corner by the bar and Ken was back at the stove. The lights were as bright as ever. One time, I dared to suggest Ken dim them to make it more romantic. Although he did it for me that night, it wasn't his standard procedure.

Shelly came over to welcome us and take our drink orders. She said, "Did you see your picture in the paper?" She was referring to our last visit there when we happened to all get our photo taken by a food reviewer. "You'll see it if you go in the bathroom."

I laughed and asked if we'd get to see Baby Ted. Ken had studied art with Ted for years and their friendship became so strong that they named their only son after him.

There were paintings similar to Ted's work around the entire restaurant. The first time I was there, Ken had asked me which one I liked the best and the one I pointed to turned out to be the only one by Ted. Ken had looked disappointed and asked, "Can you tell me what the difference is?"

I hesitated to answer but finally I said, "Perhaps, it's just the confidence in the lines? He's had so many years of experience." But I knew that there was a special energy that Ted put into his work. There was nothing wrong with Ken's paintings – they just couldn't possibly have that necessary ingredient to make it a Ted painting.

"Yes, I will bring Baby Ted down when we are finished serving," said Shelley. "He's with his Nana."

We sipped our cold drinks and looked around at the various people. There were some naval men from the nearby military base, there were young families with children, and of course, there were several couples – some who looked more in love than others. I always found myself looking at couples and watching to see how much they liked each other or if they looked bored. One man was looking at his phone, which wasn't a good sign.

Ken hurried over and with a flourish set down a plate of spring rolls. They were baked instead of deep fried. "Please try," said Ken, nodding and smiling before dashing back to the kitchen.

"Oh, good. It looks like Ken is going to do the ordering for us," I said, as I bit into a crispy roll. "Yummy."

"He always brings us extra things to taste," said Ted. "But I know I have to have the war wonton soup. Shall we get a big one?"

"No, thanks, Ted. I want to save room for Pad Thai. Or maybe I'll get the tofu with hoisin sauce." I studied the menu as Ted wolfed down the rest of the rolls.

Shelly returned and asked us what we'd like to order. "War wonton soup, of course," she said, patting Ted's shoulder.

"Yes, just a small one for me and we should get the ginger black bean snapper, don't you think, Jan?"

"Great idea."

"How about spicy coconut chicken?"

"Sure. You can take home what you don't eat."

"And you always like your Pad Thai. Do you think that will be enough?"

"Ted, we've already had spring rolls."

Ted laughed. "I could eat everything on this menu but I will resist," said Ted, passing it back to Shelly.

Ted looked around at the other guests with curiosity. "I keep forgetting it's Valentine's Day. But I see they even have some hearts decorating the window. Shall we write something about this day?"

"Of course, Ted," I said, opening my journal.

Valentine's Day

If you give and share your love, each day is precious and a tribute to St. Valentine. You cannot have a special day devoted to love because it is ever present, and its magic shapes our lives and actions because love is a unique feeling.

Where love is, anger is not. Where love is, joy prevails. So, a Valentine's Day can be repeated every day, every week and every month because love is timeless, and its boundaries are vast. There are no fences around love. All is an open gate leading to broad sunny pastures that we can wander through unhindered.

So, freedom remains a quality of love – the freedom to choose, the freedom to think the finest thoughts and noblest actions. Everyone is an aristocrat where love is concerned. Meanness and bigotry do not diminish love because love's feeling transcends them all. If we are to love our neighbour as ourselves, it's an almost impossible task because concentrated love is given to one with whom we share. This sharing is uninhibited by mean thoughts. To share is to give of oneself. This is not only a rare quality – it is a precious one. Therefore, let us continue to pay homage to St. Valentine and all he represents.

Shelly had put Ted's bowl of soup beside him while he spoke, but Ted continued to sit with a faraway look in his eyes. "Penny for your thoughts, Ted."

Ted placed the serviette in his collar and pulled the large bowl closer. "I'm not sure I even scratched the surface on that one because there's so much to say about love and sharing, and I was remembering an unpleasant bit of sharing which I don't usually do and I'd rather not discuss at the moment. Let's eat."

Ted slurped on the soup. "Why don't you try one of these wontons, dear?"

"That's okay. I find them a bit too slippery. I *am* interested in an unpleasant memory you might have, Ted. It would give me some contrast and help me see you as normal."

"Oh, I'm normal all right. As much as I wish I weren't."

Shelly set down the various beautifully-presented dishes. Ted had once explained to me that Ken had studied with a French chef somewhere along the way.

We both loaded up our plates, and were soon lost in a world of delicious smells and tastes.

Partway through our meal, Ken came over and asked how everything was. Ted's mouth was full so he just gave the okay sign. I asked Ken if the lime leaves had been used for years in his culture or if it was more of a recent trend.

"Yes, we have used for years – do you like?"

"I sure do," I said. "This snapper is heavenly."

Ken grinned, gave Ted an affectionate pat on his shoulder, and dashed back to his station.

Sated, Shelly took away the leftovers to be put in take-out containers and we sat sipping Chinese tea. I didn't try to make conversation with Ted. He seemed lost in thought as he rested his delicate hands around the warm cup. I smiled as I watched a baby sucking on a bottle with a look of bliss on his face. We humans only require a warm room and good food to feel contentment.

"Let's write a poem about People, shall we?" said Ted.

By the time I found my journal, Ted was speaking.

People

Of all the animals in the world, people are the most numerous and they have power, especially when they are united. This power is for good or evil and can be manipulated by a leader who is chosen by the people to express their views to the outside world. This leads to a benign dictatorship or a wicked self-seeking dictatorship – whose leader has the power to seduce the people towards his way of thinking. The Nazis, who fell, 'hook, line and sinker', for the leadership of Adolf Hitler best illustrate this. Hitler seduced them carefully and gained their trust, and then, after gaining power, he rewrote the laws to suit himself. For a law-abiding people, this was very dangerous because unwittingly, they managed to enslave themselves with a tangle of laws, which they felt they could not break.

So, we must beware of to whom we give power because having great powers can corrupt even good people and ipso facto the people then become enslaved to the leaders. In our democracy, we are blessed with the means of getting rid of a party or a leader who is voted into power by un-voting them in the next election. Thus, democracy tends to keep leaders incorruptible. We are all on a ship of state together and it behooves us not to rock the boat too much. Luckily, before it capsizes, we hold an election, and change the captain and crew. Heaven help us if we couldn't do this because a mutiny could be termed unpatriotic. We must start in the schools by teaching children the benefits of our system and the benefit of being a democracy. Otherwise, a demagogue could lead them astray.

Fortunately, in Canada, our system of government seems to work towards stability and unlike many countries, it functions well when considering the size of the country, where some provinces are greater in area than many countries of the world. That is what makes Canada such a great place to live in because we have a lot of space and good government to keep peace and order throughout the territory.

As I put the journal aside, I couldn't resist saying, "Ted, you don't really think Harper isn't corrupt, do you? I mean, just compare him for a moment to Obama and there's such a striking difference in every way."

"You're quite right, my dear, and I *am* grateful that I got to see a wonderful president such as Obama come into power. Unlike Harper, he does truly care about the people. He will go down in history as a man of judgement, compassion and intelligence."

"And it doesn't hurt that he's so darn handsome," I added.

"Of course, the ladies appreciate that," agreed Ted.

Ken came over with two small plates and placed them in front of us. "Deep fried bananas. Please enjoy."

Although we were both full, we dug in with enthusiasm. The crowd was thinning, so Ken pulled a chair over to join us.

"Ted, are you still thinking of painting a mural on the wall?" asked Ken.

Ted pushed the empty plate away. "As a matter of fact, I was just thinking about that. Since you have so much fish on the menu, we will have to have a water theme with lots of colourful fish."

"What can I do to make it easier for you?"

"Well, perhaps we can do it together. I can't really stand so unless we do a Michelangelo with scaffolding and me lying under the ceiling …"

"That's a good idea," said Ken. "It could be on the ceiling."

Ted discarded that thought with a wave of his hands. "No, no, I'm thinking it would be like old times if we worked together. I can be sitting down doing everything within reach and you can do the higher parts. It will be a collaboration."

"What a wonderful idea," I said excitedly. "Ken, which wall are you thinking?"

Ken pointed to a wall that was painted red. "And would you keep the red as a backdrop?" I asked.

Ted shrugged and said, "Sure, why not. Who said water has to be blue."

Shelly arrived and put Baby Ted on Ted's lap. The child cuddled close to Ted's large belly. Ted held him gently and talked nonsense to him to make him laugh. Baby Ted was holding a toy car and after a short time, he wiggled to get on the floor and play with it at our feet.

"He's growing up fast, Ken," said Ted. "Soon, he'll be learning to cook as well as you can."

"No," said Ken. "I want him to go to university and do what he believes in, whatever that is."

Shelly stood and watched proudly before she went to settle a bill at one of the remaining tables.

"Ted, should we make a date for starting our project?" asked Ken.

Ted sat and pondered, and I said, "In case you want to start on Sunday, I'm playing at the church next door for the next three Sundays and I'm there for about three hours in the morning. I notice you don't open on Sundays, Ken. So, if you want to start early, I can pick you up at 9 a.m., Ted."

"Good Lord. That's early. I'll be on my fifth yawn at that hour."

"That would work out well for us," said Ken. "Why don't you think about it, Ted, and let me know." He lifted Baby Ted and put him on his knee. "Baby Ted would love to have you here." Turning to me, he said, "Do you play at that church often?"

"No, just a few times a year. I substitute for different United Church musicians when they can't be there or are on holidays. It's rather a coincidence that it's this one coming up."

Later, as I was pulling the car into the underground parkade at Sunrise, Ted said, "You know, I would love to do that mural but when we originally talked about it, I was much stronger. Now my spirit is willing but... I hate to disappoint him."

"I'm sure he would understand if you bailed, Ted, but maybe you could just get him started on doing his own thing. He needs to believe in himself."

"That's a good idea."

I parked by the elevator door and helped Ted get out. "You *will* come up for a short good-night won't you, Darling."

"I'll make sure you're safe. I don't know why we didn't take your walker, Ted. Sorry, I'm oblivious at times."

"No, you're not," he said, leaning on my arm.

Once we were inside his room, he hurled himself into his chair. "It's so peaceful here, isn't it? And it's so nice to be out of that wind and rain."

Just then, a woman came into the room with his pills, dispelling the peace idea. She gave him a small paper cup with mashed up pills, and he made a face as he tossed them back.

I sat on the couch thinking about what I was going to do when I got home. I kept my coat on and my purse on my lap intending to get going, but Ted had different ideas.

"Oh, here's the heart you brought me. Will you have a bite?"

I waved it away, holding my full tummy, but Ted took a large bite from it.

"Purdies are damn good." After licking his chocolatey lips, he said, "One more poem, Jan, please. You and I never talk about the weather, since we have more important things to discuss but it's time we said something about it."

I could see that Ted was wide awake so I dug in my bag for the old journal.

The Weather

I am a person of varied moods, and I have observed that when the sun is shining and the birds are singing and the flowers are blooming, I feel like blooming. I feel like singing and dancing.

Then, the weather changes. The other day, it was drizzling all day – wet and damp – and my spirits dropped. The whole world looked wet and damp. No blue sky – joyless – until the following day, when the sun broke through and made us feel better.

Even in the dead of winter in the Yukon, the sun shines. The birds don't sing because they mostly all migrate south – except for the crows and ravens – they stay with mankind even on the coldest of days. A snowy day can be quite uplifting because everything becomes pure white. The sky is white and the ground is white, and white means purity. Angels wear robes of white. You never see an angel in black. Yet, ravens and crows wear black, and they're so faithful to man – they hang around through the winter no matter what. And, like man, they are very intelligent, but they use their intelligence in a creative way in order to prolong and guard their species.

We can even feel happy in the coldest weather, providing we have our furs and parkas on hand. Weather is like our personality – ever-changing – for good or bad. But we cannot say weather is evil unless it runs amok like when we have sudden storms and hurricanes. Then, the weather can be evil and injurious. Even the rain, if it's heavy, can change the lives of people and animals. So, one must seek for a delicate balance between weather and goodwill. Our friends, the Americans, are dropping various chemicals in order to stop the earth from becoming too warm but one person's 'too warm' is another person's pleasant weather. So, we must take the weather when it comes and if it gets really vicious, we must seek protection from it.

The person who loves the sea and admires it from the land can change their tune once they're on the ocean experiencing the thrill of a storm with a latent danger that they could sink in it.

So, we can agree that weather is like people – smiling and beneficent or raging, and cold and cruel. We are creatures of nature and so is our weather. We are doomed to live together in harmony or suffer the worst.

"Interesting that you get into weather while thinking about Valentine's Day," I said, standing up and throwing my purse over my shoulder. "You covered a lot of territory in that one – even American politics."

"I never really know what will come out. Thank you so much for a delightful evening, once again. I love you, you darling girl."

I leaned down to give him a long hug and kiss. "I love *you!* And you're right chipper, Ted, for such a rainy night."

While riding down the elevator, I started to smile, picturing Ted lying on a scaffold painting the ceiling of Ken's restaurant.

Boobs and the Heart

I plodded through the mushy chestnut leaves on the sidewalk of busy Shelbourne Street towards Ted's latest abode called Parkwood. I hadn't seen Ted in weeks. I knew he wouldn't understand what I was going through since I didn't understand it myself. I had suddenly become sensitive to electromagnetic smog and there was no escaping it. I had been researching it and some people called it Radar sickness.

Even though I owned a lovely condo, I couldn't stay there because it had more of that than I could handle. Living there I became ill and confused. For the last four months, I had slept in friends' basements and attics, and camped in various parks, unable to work and wondering where I would find a place I could relax in. The previous month, I had run into Artie at the graveyard we used to walk through together. We hadn't seen each other in a year. He convinced me to come see his psychologist with him, who explained to me that because Artie had Post Traumatic Stress from a terrible accident he had been in the year before, he was probably not going to ever be able to have a relationship in the normal way. She said that Art was pretty amazing the way he had continued with his business as a tour guide, and he was learning to control his anger and stress. As she described his symptoms, I was shocked to realize she was describing me. I seemed to have PTSD as a result of the shocks I had encountered at the condo. I had always been sensitive but this experience had shattered me. Too much WIFI, smart meters and radar. I had described it to myself as a nervous breakdown.

I was now living in Artie's third wheel on a remote beach. He was kind enough to suggest it, as the place was surrounded by cliffs and had no cell reception. Art didn't visit me there as it was too far out of town. I was currently the only one in the private campground. The weather had changed and the park would be closing in two more weeks, so I would have to find a new place to live while I waited for the condo to sell in a deflated market. The night before a torrential rain and wind had caused part of the cliff behind me to slide down, and I wished it had buried me. Suicide was on my mind a lot. I knew Ted was going through depression too. He had gotten sick and when he came to, he found himself in a high-care facility for very demented patients. His first words to me then had been, "Who did this to me? Was it my son?" I explained that Charles had done all that he could from Toronto and that he had assumed Ted needed full-time care since he was out of it for a couple of weeks. This was the only place that was available at the time.

I punched in the code to enter the front door of the nursing home, signed myself in and punched in another code to open the door to the stairwell. Ted was definitely the most with-it resident in this locked ward of highly disfunctional patients. He lived on the second floor above the front entrance, beside the nursing office. I ran up the stairs and pushed another button to unlock the door at the top. All doors had to be coded so the residents couldn't wander and get lost. In the hall sat four residents talking to themselves, nervously wringing their hands, or pleading for someone to listen to them. They ignored each other. I gave a forced smile. When I opened the door, I was surprised to see Ted in his bed which was like a hospital bed. The metal sides were pulled up so that he was cribbed in. His head was propped up so that he could watch the television that was always on.

"Hello, Ted," I said as I leaned in to give him a kiss. "Why are you in bed so early?"

"Oh, I think they put me here because they want to get their chores done early. Turn off the TV, would you?"

As I did, I said, "They know you can't keep falling asleep in your wheelchair. That's hard on your neck." His La-Z-Boy was turned to face the wall so that it couldn't be used. They had once found him sprawled on the floor below it, when he was trying to wiggle into a more comfortable position. "I'll write to Barry. They should be able to find you an alternative. To only have a wheelchair and bed to choose from is ridiculous." As I said that, I realized how quickly this wonderful man had lost his independence. It was a lesson – it could well happen to any of us.

"Charles was here a few days ago. He was with a different woman."

"Did you like her? What was she like?"

"She was much younger – they're never older women. But actually, I did like her. I hope Charles can make this one work."

"Were they in Victoria long?"

"I don't know, but they just visited the once I think. He brought me a new wheel chair."

I went over to look at it. "This is nice and light, Ted. It will be way easier to take you for a walk."

"I don't think I want to go outside."

"You always say that but once you're outside, you love it. You must have been happy to see Charles after all these months."

Ted's blue eyes sparkled at me behind his clear spectacles. "I'm so happy to see you, dear. Where have you been? Have you been working a lot?"

For the first time, I lied to Ted. Nodding my head, I said, "You know how busy things get at the beginning of the school year."

Ted stared at me, as if he knew I wasn't telling him the truth. "Can you get me out of here?"

"I wish I could, Ted. But they even use that big machine to lift you onto the toilet. I guess you don't have any muscle strength after what you've been through. Why are the sides of the bed up? Are they afraid you'll fall out?"

"All I know is, there's no way I'll have any women visitors in my bed."

"Screw that," I said, my devilish side finally kicking in. I took off my shoes and climbed in beside him. Cuddling against him, I said, "Tell me a story."

Ted immediately responded in the same vein. "Once upon a time, a beautiful blonde princess flew to my window. 'Let me in, kind sir,' she pleaded. I asked if I could pull on her boob to pull her onto my bed."

"Ow, that must have hurt," I muttered.

Ted reached over to touch my breast. "How beautiful," he sighed. He touched his own breast. "Feel this – it's absolutely boring, right?"

I rested my hand on his chest. "It's part of you, Ted, so I wouldn't say that."

"The design of a male breast cannot compare to that of a woman." He rested his hand on my breast again. I noticed that I felt no reaction to this unusual behaviour from Ted. Not even embarrassment. Just a mild curiosity. "Mankind has always had a fascination with breasts, and they come in so many different sizes and shapes. You see, it conjures up so many comforting memories – perhaps of our mother, or our lovers, or our wives as mothers. And, of course, if the hormones are in good working order, it can stimulate wonderful sensations for both parties, especially during love-making."

I relaxed beside Ted, and felt deep compassion for this wonderful man who was so deprived of physical and emotional contact. And I had failed him over the past few weeks. I thought about my time years before as a nurse's aide at Wayside House – a Christian Science Nursing Home. There, because no medications were used to dull the pain, we knew how important it was to provide loving touches as we helped the residents with their care. I remembered crouching down beside the bed in my favourite lady's room – Mrs. Lawrence – in case my Supervisor came looking for me. I loved hearing her stories and making her laugh. If my Supervisor came in, I'd be out of sight and we'd giggle after she left. But now, with the new technology to help nurse's backs, feeble residents were deprived of physical touch.

Ted said, "Jan, you are at the same time very naive and very experienced. As a man, I've had so many lovers I couldn't begin to count them. I know you're not like that but you are very experienced for a woman."

"The funny thing is that it's seems it took half my life, and a few partners for me to really understand and enjoy my sexuality. I would say Artie has been the ultimate in that department."

I sat up and climbed out of the bed. "Ted, we haven't written anything down in ages. Perhaps, you could emote about something you've been thinking about as you lie here. Do you reminisce or do you mostly sleep?"

"I don't remember right now. But I know what we should write about, since we're talking about breasts."

"Strip clubs?"

"Pigs."

I laughed, and realized it was the first time I had laughed in weeks. I surely did love this man. I found a piece of paper and pen under a pile of magazines.

Pigs

When I see a pig, visions of motherhood come to my mind. The huge, plump, pink pig, with oodles of teats hanging invitingly from her tummy while her piglets answer the invitation by rushing up and grabbing a teat in their tiny mouths. The mother lies down and a regimented row of piglets slurp, slurp, suck, suck, munch, munch contentedly on each teat while the mother seems to snore comfortably.

I once saw a huge pig sunbathing on top of a pile of manure. It epitomized all that was good about manure and sunbathing. I believe they *do* get sunburned and they can go a fiery pink with the sun's rays. However, this one made no move to move and just stayed in the sunlight. Its body language showed joy and contentment in a pig's paradise. It did not care that it would end up as rashers of bacon and smoked hams. Perhaps, it was dreaming of having the whole pigswill to itself. But it gave me pause to think how rapturously content a pig can be without television, radio, jazz bands or symphonies. They just enjoy lying in the sun. The only time life is not a bore is when the boar appears. But it doesn't faze the fat pig that takes everything in her stride.

Let us learn from pigs – how to live a calm, contented life. Of course, we would have to discard our imagination because we would have to know there were hundreds of frying pans waiting to greet us on hot stoves. I feel sorry for vegetarians because to them, a sizzling rasher is unknown. The joys of Pogrom are transmitted to the human through tasting that beautiful body that lay sunbathing on the manure pile. I think there should be a monument to pigs because they really enrich our tables and our lives. The mother feeding her brood is soon to become a roasted chunk of pork on the dinner table. Oh, what a delightful scent is roast piggy. Pigs are like walking menus and at their lives' end, they will have contributed to enriching the lives of humans.

I put the paper aside and watched Ted lying there, his body so still but his face alive with wisdom and curiosity. "Speaking of boobs, Ted, I was thinking about how they are simply the covering of the most important organ in our body. There are people in spiritual communities that believe that the more positive and generous you can allow yourself to be, the stronger the vibrations are from your heart. And these protect you from just about anything."

As I said this, I thought about how I had virtually shut mine down as I hid away from all that seemed to bother me at the time. My fear was certainly not going to allow my heart to do its job and I might as well be dead if I didn't allow my heart to do all that it was meant to do. My Quantum Healing studies needed to be dusted off because we had learned that in the first hour of lessons.

"Yes, I watched a show about the frequencies from the loving heart. We just assume that if we can't see it, it's not important," said Ted.

"I have a friend who uses dousing rods pointed at the heart to show how you open or close them with your thinking. It's fascinating."

"I'd like to see that," said Ted. "Bring some next time. Shall we write about the subject?"

The Heart

The heart can be part of your anatomy but it is often used to symbolize love in the purest sense – love, which gives and does not count the cost; love, which transforms and creates a beautiful spirit from one that was more mundane.

Lovers cut hearts on trees and pierce them with little arrows, emulating Cupid. Cupid was a servant of the goddess of love, and he ran around shooting arrows into lovers and blending their love together so that they became one. This is the idea behind marriage. But it doesn't work all the time. In fact, it amazes me that people still support marriage – because marriage is really a gamble. You see the horse and bet on it, but in the race, it stumbles and never reaches the finish line. Whereas if you let the horse go, you're free to try another horse and so love can carry on quite well without being tied down.

The heart is very sensitive to rejection. There is many a dear lover who has committed suicide because their dream has not turned out to be one of reality. The wonderful thing is that if you give your heart to someone and they respond, there is often a great welding of spirit and this weld can last for many, many years. Because love is like good wine that matures over time, becoming richer and more fruitful. It becomes a strong force for good, reaching the highest human aspiration. Amor vincit omnia (love conquers all).

I lay the paper aside and sat thinking about what we had discussed here and how I felt more grounded and relaxed than I had in the last few months. Maybe it was enough to focus on the heart, while in the company of someone you love, to activate it fully. Most people would think I was crazy.

A girl came in and when she saw me, she giggled and told Ted she would give him a little more time before she prepared him for sleep. "He doesn't get enough visitors," she said.

"You probably feel more like getting up for breakfast than going to sleep, eh, Ted?" I asked.

"As you know, I have amazing dreams in technicolour so it's actually one of the best parts of the day. I used to love going for meals but I dread it here."

"I know, Ted. It must be depressing but I'm so glad you have that wonderful man from Nepal that looks after you in the dining room."

"Ah yes, I forget his name, but that's a man with an open heart. You know, dear, I'm hoping I don't have to be here for much longer. I wish I weren't so darn healthy."

"I've had that feeling," I said, not telling him how recent it was.

"One more poem, Jan."

The Joys of Paradise

The other night, I dreamt I died. It was extremely pleasant as I floated as a spirit, my body long since having been destroyed. But my body was still so free. Just as Plato said – it's the Spirit that lives on. It was a pleasant death because I did not meet any relatives or people who had controlled my life in the past. However, I did meet my wife and we enjoyed a beer together before entering the pearly gates.

I know there is a pub outside the Pearly Gates run by a Scots woman. I didn't stay too long in that pub because I wanted to explore paradise and meet all the beautiful maids who circled around there. Perhaps, heaven is full of prostitutes. If so, it would be rather interesting to see how they have changed their characters. Anyway, I found death to be another adventure in life. There were so many good people there that it was like Hell. They were singing hymns and making a terrific racket. I reluctantly returned to Earth and decided to wait a few years before sampling more of the joys of paradise.

I rested my hands lightly on Ted's shoulders and forced myself to make eye contact. He studied me thoughtfully with his piercing eyes. I wished I could explain why I was so anxious. I knew my shoulders were up around my ears and I had shallow breathing. I was on high alert and tuned into what felt like a lot of Wi-Fi. The aides' office was next door so maybe I was feeling something there. But I was also dreading the long drive back to the Beachcomber campground. It might be weeks before I managed another trip to see Ted, even though my time with him felt like a priority. Ted seemed to watch the thoughts swirling in my head. He reached for my hand. I felt the tremor that was constant in his hand but I also felt a beautiful strength. If Ted could handle his hardships, I could certainly handle mine. I gave him a kiss and quickly went out the door before he saw my tears.

Winning and Losing

I lifted out my bag of goodies from the trunk of the car in the basement of Parkwood. I knew I wouldn't be able to get Ted outside on a rainy day like today but I figured we could have a little party in his room. I needed to celebrate the fact that I was slowly recovering from what seemed to have been a mental breakdown and severe depression. And hopefully, I would someday be free of my sensitivity.

Something had made me answer an odd ad on Used Victoria when I was living on the beach in a trailer. The ad said they wanted someone to live in the house they had bought in the Uplands until they retired from Vancouver. And they wanted to be able to come and stay there on the occasional weekend. The rent was reasonable but I had to consider that I would need to move again in eight months with my grand piano. I had phoned them from a pay phone at the trailer park on the beach, since there was no cell reception. After a long talk, and putting a pile of coins in for the long-distance call, I knew I liked the woman on the other end of the phone and she seemed to feel the same way. And now, two months later, I was in their lovely home and they had already come to stay a couple of times – two women, a social worker and a psychologist, who were compassionate, fun-loving and who supported the arts. They were supportive of my medical condition. They were curious about the special tent with metal threads that covered my bed and impressed that it protected me from the electromagnetic smog that was now everywhere. I still didn't sleep very well with all the vibrations I felt but at least I could stop being on the alert. I was so grateful to have

Roz and Kathy in my life, and looked forward to sharing food, wine and laughter with them on their monthly visits.

Ted looked up from the TV when I walked in. He was missing his sparkle but he said, "It's you. Where have you been?"

"Oh, Ted, it's a long story," I said, setting the bag down and bending to hug him. "I've sure missed you. What are you watching?"

"Nothing much. That seems to be the only station that has the subtitles and I have to put up with a lot of drivel. Turn it off, please."

Because I didn't have a TV, I lingered for a few minutes, watching a boat going through some everglades. "Hey, look at all the butterflies. We don't seem to have very many anymore."

I turned off the TV and opened a big bag of chips. "Would you like a Guinness, or some of this mango juice?"

"The juice would be nice."

"And I also brought some chocolate covered ginger and cashews I made for a party I'm going to tomorrow."

"Whose party?" asked Ted, digging into the bag of chips.

"Believe it or not, I got involved with a meditation group that I just love. Everyone is so positive and fun. Of course, most of them are women. We're having a potluck tomorrow."

I opened a cider for myself and drank from the can. I was drinking more than usual these days but it seemed to help ground me. I told myself I was self-medicating. We both crunched on some chips. Ted started to perk up.

"Have you had some interesting visitors lately?" I asked.

"Not that I remember. I think you said you moved. Are you missing that beautiful condo?"

I still didn't feel I could tell Ted about my health but I hadn't had a great experience with some of the residents so I decided to share a bit.

"Not at all, Ted. I didn't tell you what happened before I put it on the market. It made it much easier to sign the contract."

Ted shakily lifted the glass to his lips, and after taking a sip, he said, "Oh lovely. What happened?"

"The police knocked on my door. I was entertaining Artie at the time."

"Artie? I thought you two ended that again?"

"I know, we have a record for the most break-ups of any relationship, I'm sure. We really aren't terribly compatible, but we respect each other and we've got that crazy chemistry."

"I think I know what you mean. Like I've always said, you're not the type to have a normal relationship."

"Are you saying I'm abnormal?" I teased. I crossed my legs and tried to get comfortable on the straight dining room chair that was the only thing available for a guest to sit on. It would seem guests weren't encouraged to visit for long. Or maybe it was just that the room was smaller than the one at Sunrise and needed to have space for the large machine used to lift Ted.

"Yes, I am, actually," said Ted. "But what did the police want?"

"They came in and sat down – a woman and a man – and said my next-door neighbours had called to say all her jewellery was missing. Worth over $100,000 according to appraisals. And I was the only one with a key to the place while they were away. I was shocked that they wouldn't come to me first. I was their friend. I'd had them over for drinks and meals, and taken them for drives. They were an older couple that I really liked and they gave me a key to use while they were in their home in Mexico, where they winter every year. I just went in once a week or so to pile their mail away and make sure everything looked normal. I admit I was surprised they chose me to do that since they'd live in the building for years and had only known me for a few months."

Ted was frowning. His glasses had slid to the bottom of his nose and he peered at me over them. "How could they possibly think you were a thief? You're a generous person."

"The police were very nice and said that because of her age, they suspected she had forgotten where she had hidden it and they wanted me to write a report from my side of it."

Ted continued to munch chips, watching me intently. I knew he was probably having trouble hearing me but he got the gist of it. The front of his stained red sweater was covered in crumbs. "Bloody Hell. What a thing to go through."

"And worst of all, they interrogated Artie who was visiting me there for the first time. And the people that lived in the condo were very cold to me in my last days there. It made me glad to leave."

"Why didn't you tell me this before? No wonder you haven't been yourself."

"It just got sorted out recently. The police forwarded me a letter from my neighbour apologizing that she had found her jewellery behind her yoga mat in the closet, where she never would have put it. It frosts me that she didn't even look everywhere possible. I've been stewing about this for months. And no attempt to repair the damage she's done to me. Or to write to me directly."

"Maybe you should sue her for defamation of character and for causing stress."

I looked down at my hands and realized I was literally wringing them. "I'm sure she's embarrassed. Ted, since I got involved in this meditation group, I realize how important it is to focus on the positive side of life and let the other stuff go. And maybe all this happened so that I would have a bit of a spiritual awakening. Does that make sense? Have you ever felt like you had something terrible happen to you but because of it, you were led to find something wonderful?"

"Probably. I can't think of anything at the moment." Ted turned his head to look out the narrow window. All that could be seen was the top of the glass roof over the front door and a portion of the large chestnut tree on the street.

"Maybe I'm crazy but my theory is that the only reason we have disasters happen is so that we go somewhere we never would have gone before, or stop doing something that isn't good for us or the planet. We're forced to take a new direction and that causes us to meet people we needed to meet. Like this meditation group – I could never get into meditation before I met them but I was feeling a bit desperate. It's not a religion but it feels like we're having an elevated experience when we all tune in together. It's a harmony, in a way. I've had the same thing happen as a jazz musician, when I play with masterful people that don't have big egos."

"Life does not have to be as difficult as some people make it out to be. Our thinking plays a large part."

"Why don't we write down something about this subject, Ted?" I asked as I pulled my journal from my purse.

Winning and Losing

Life is a gamble. There are winners and losers. But it's better to be a winner most of the time and lose only a few objects in life, and the winning is not always material – neither is the losing. We can win an ambition and often lose an aim in life. However, if we learn by our losing, we can also learn by our winning and the two ultimately balance out.

We can win friends and we can win enemies or we can lose both – it all depends on the throw of life's dice. People often love someone so dearly – yet, the feeling is not reciprocated so they lose heart or they can even lose a love of life because they have put too much of their feelings with just one person.

In order to be happy, we must love the world and all its facets – the adventure of just living is enough to keep one on one's toes and each day should bring a new joy in life – whether it be a glorious morning sunrise or the breeze rustling through the nearby trees. Then comes a placid afternoon which tapers away to an evening of relaxation and meditation, and we create the good feelings in our minds, and I may say, the bad feelings also. So, it is up to us, personally, to discipline our thoughts, which are like the ocean. They can be tumultuous and rough, or placid and calm. Our bodies must dance to the rhythm of life in a positive way. It is fatal to blow ones' top over tiny things, whereas the disciplined mind will train the mind so that it is not destructive. We should aspire to love all that is positive in life, including love itself.

Life may be a gamble but it is a gamble we can win with the right thought. If we give up hope, our joy will recede because joy and hope walk hand in hand in life. You can't buy joy with cash but you can spend the cash wisely to help fulfill your aims – which bring joy. And the one thing you have to have faith in, is your own ability to surmount problems and negative thoughts. Music can dispel negative thoughts if it is of the right type. For instance, Beethoven can bring you to tears with his chords. So can simple folk tunes because, being uncomplicated, they help the mind to rest. The cacophony of popular music can coarsen the senses, and generally weaken one's personality and aims. The screeching of popular songs and the blaring of popular digital music just deforms the senses. There is nothing more destructive than a screeching, unmusical noise, combined with ungrammatical words which distort both good English and good taste. Youth are attracted by this element in modern 'music' because it is rebellious and against tradition. If we follow this unrestrained taste, we are losing the finer points of our being. Rebelliousness may be good in politics, but it can be destructive to the aesthetic feelings of humanity.

Of course, any creative endeavour can uphold the finer points of life or negate their influence for good by a cacophonous noise or a coarseness of thought. Most young people are very sensitive to the criticism of their peers and therefore, hide their real preferences in order not to endure the criticism of their friends. However, we must all follow our true aims and nature to be independent of official taste.

We do not lose out if we follow our true instinct and cleave to that which is positive and good in our lives. Most people fail to see how strong their influence can be so we sing the same hymns, mumble the same prayers and follow the same teachings which are fed to us by the same authorities who themselves are comforted by the status quo, and do not trespass into any new thoughts but we must always aim for that which will improve our lives and the lives of others. That is why life is like a tightrope and as we walk along the tightrope, we can often feel it wiggle under our feet so we must keep our balance in our points of view, which should be positive.

Everyone is their own captain on the boat of life and we must develop the skills which enable us to stay on course – not to panic – not to fret – not to make sudden changes – but to forge ahead, protected by our knowledge of what is best as we head for the unknown shores of the future.

I polished off my cider and laughed. "I think you pretty much summed up what we were talking about and then some. Tell me, do you have any theories about why some people seem to have so many more hardships than others. Do you think most people bring it on themselves?"

"Are you referring to karma? All I know is that the more you can stop the fearful monkey brain, the calmer you are. I'm glad you're meditating. It allows you to make choices carefully."

"You're being polite, Ted. You could easily accuse me of rushing into things without thinking. I've made some rash decisions and they were motivated by fear."

"You're not unusual in that regard, my dear. Let's change the subject. When you first came in you mentioned a subject that I'd like to ponder."

Butterflies

The butterflies have gone. They were here yesterday, flitting over the flowers and sipping the nectar, and today they're gone. They have gone to Mexico. They fly up into the sky, and join their comrades in the hundreds and thousands, all flying to Mexico. They go there because it's warm there. The sun shines far warmer there than in Canada.

They have their own secret travel agencies and off they go with very little luggage. Whereas we must go through customs and carry passports – all the impedimenta that we humans must carry. In Mexico, we try out our Spanish: Como esta usted? But the butterflies don't speak Spanish. However, they still enjoy the thrill of being in Mexico and they find the same friendly flowers they found in the North. Big pink and rosy red flowers attract them.

What do they do in Mexico? The one thing they were born for. To practice sex 'neath the warm Mexican sun and then lay millions upon millions of eggs, and from these eggs, millions more caterpillars emerge. The caterpillar forms a cocoon and later emerges as a second generation of butterflies, only to go to Mexico again for the sex orgy. They don't even read a book. They don't even use condoms. They just enjoy sex and then they die. What a life.

I do not want to be a butterfly. Everything is so brief. You haven't time to savour the good life but you *do* see the world.

Ted tried to move himself in the wheelchair. No doubt his bottom was sore. "Did I hear you mention Guinness earlier?" he asked.

"Yes, I thought there was something wrong with you when you opted for juice," I said, pulling one from my bag. "I found some smaller bottles rather than those big cans. You should be able to manage one of these." I poured it into a glass and smiled when he held it up to look at the foamy head with delight.

"I nearly forgot how much I enjoy this."

"It probably has been a few months since you've had one, Ted. I'm so glad you're feeling better."

"So tell me about where you're living now."

"I'm hoping you can come and visit me there, Ted. There are four or five steps so we should wait to do it when Barry is visiting. And I hope you can meet the ladies that own it."

"You like them?"

"Yes, they're so special. The first weekend they came, I suggested I make them dinner. We opened wine and shared food, and talked so easily and laughed a lot. We got up the next morning, and walked to Estevan village for breakfast and back through the Uplands woods."

"I'd like to meet them," said Ted.

"To top it off, they have a fabulous art collection. I was telling them a little about our relationship and the next time they came, they brought a painting by you for me to enjoy while I'm there. Now it's the first thing I see when I open the front door."

"Yes, I do need to meet them. Which painting is it?"

"It's medium size – a snowy scene with a woman and two children walking, and a black cat just behind them. There's a wonky house and two canoes upside down. And of course, a raven is flying. It's you, and I love living with it."

"I wish I could still paint," said Ted.

I opened the chocolates and had one. "If I was here to help you, do you think you would like to try it again?"

"I don't think I would be happy with the results." He looked across the room at one of the first paintings he had done. It was of the mining town he was raised in and it was very un-Ted-like, with muted colours, and realistic images.

"Hey, Ted, I don't think you've ever had me write down something about artists. Feel like giving it a try?"

Painting

I see the distant hills rising and falling in one gigantic rhythm, so I paint their outlines and my brush caresses the canvas. They are dead until the colour comes into my mind. Let's make them red. Let's make them blue. Let's make them pink. With every hue, at last, I'm in the world of paint, and reality disappears. The world is now my creation. I move mountains. I form lakes and valleys. Rivers pour over the heights down into the canvas and soon, I have created my own small world. Then, I can place a sun in the sky – or a moon. Whatever takes my fancy.

The huge ball of the sun gives light to the canvas and to this world. It is a symbol of the universe, and yet, we are so small and insignificant when seen from far outer space. This world is so big to us – so great and magnificent – and yet, to the general universe, it is unknown and heated by a small star. Yet, we thrive in our miniscule universe. Our nearest neighbours are millions of miles from us and we are lost in the maelstrom of eternity.

Our puny wars and struggles are meaningless to the rest of nature. The creation of God is such a small affair amidst the whole universe and yet, we have existed for millions of years. Long before man came on the earth or living things – and here we are today still encircling the sun and heading for an unknown future. Were we to realize our destiny we would tremble with fear. A little freak of nature could consume us in a short time. The tiny band of oxygen and air is so thin and puny compared to other natural waves. All our creations – magnificent though they are – are doomed to destruction, eroded by time, and war and pestilence.

Let us be like the birds and sing while we can. Our brief lives can capture pockets of happiness and store them like the squirrel's horde. We depend upon water, air and sunlight to live – and this too could disappear, and leave no trace that humanity ever occupied this world.

"That was a bit depressing, Ted. I think you need a chocolate," I said, passing him the container. "You know I was just thinking about that painting at my house – it's rather interesting that you would choose a black cat to be there. Most people consider black cats to be bad luck – and yet they're so dramatic looking, especially with snow as the backdrop."

"I don't worry about that kind of thinking."

"Remember Val that came with me to visit you and brought her labradoodle with her – Finnegan?"

"Vaguely."

"Well, she said she had been with a man for a short time and wasn't sure she should be getting married to him, so on the day of her wedding, she asked the Universe to have a black cat run in front of her if she wasn't supposed to marry him. She said not one, but three black cats ran across the road in front of her car."

"Really? Did she marry him?"

"Yes, unfortunately. She said it was the worst two years of her life."

The door opened and the nurse walked in. She was a delicate woman who looked like she was from India. She gasped when she saw Ted. "Oh my goodness – are those potato chips you're eating, Ted?" She looked at me sternly but I could tell she was amused.

"They're jolly good and the beer is even better," said Ted.

"You do know that he has trouble swallowing, don't you, dear?" she asked me.

"I know how to do the Heimlich maneuver," I said.

Ted shouted with laughter. He waved a chip at the woman. "Don't blame her. I beg her to bring me things that crunch. The food here is like baby food."

She took Ted's arm and checked his blood pressure. "Okay, Ted, but don't overdo it." She smiled at me. "I can't be angry – I'm so happy to see Ted laugh. We all love Ted and he's been very unhappy. I hope you come back soon, but bring something healthy."

"Of course," I agreed. "I'll bring apples next time."

Ted rolled his eyes.

"It's almost time for dinner, Ted," she said as she closed the door behind her.

"Bring me apple cider," said Ted.

We both grinned at each other like two kids conspiring.

He wiggled in his chair again and sat quietly for a moment. "You know, today I was thinking about my childhood. Algar visited me last night."

Algar was Ted's twin sister who had passed away several years previously. Some people thought his reference to visits from her showed signs of dementia, but who were they to say what happens after the body dies? Maybe Ted did get visits. If it gave him comfort, I wasn't going to correct him. "What did she say?"

"Oh, I can't remember exactly. I just know I was thrilled to see her. She was such a fun playmate when we were kids. We saw some dreadful things during the war but we still managed to enjoy ourselves. I'd like to speak about that."

War

In my childhood, I saw from the bedroom window the earth light up with flares from droning bombers, which flew over our house, enlivening what could have been a quiet night. The staccato roar of Heinkel bombers filled the sky with sound and then the music changed to a heavy drumming as the bombs fell. I watched the brief flashes of light caused by the explosions as I stood fascinated at the window.

The following day, my mother took me to the town to shop but the main store had disappeared during the night leaving a guttered shell. So, it remained a cheap shopping trip, as we couldn't spend anything. No good came of it.

War is absolutely stupid. People are killed for no apparent reason. Babies die, their little lives cut short and youngsters never grow into old men and women. War hurts the innocent. The targets are killed willy-nilly, whether they be highly intelligent or not. Destruction is a play of mankind at its worst. Others may wave flags and shout for joy at the thought of a battle but only when it's far removed from the person – like some video game.

Peace can be so boring but how better to have a century of peace than a year of war.

Ted looked outside but didn't seem to notice that it was almost dark. He looked over at me and seemed surprised to see me there. "Are you teaching today?"

"No, Ted, it's Friday. I'm just going to practise the piano a bit and answer some emails I'm behind on."

"Oh Lord, I'm so glad I don't have to worry about that sort of thing."

An aide came in to take Ted for dinner. I just had time to give him a quick hug before he was wheeled across the hall to join his fellow residents. I must admit, I couldn't bring myself to join Ted over there. The few times I had done that, I had felt so phony trying to make light of a terrible situation. I gathered my things and pressed the code numbers to take the stairs down to the car park.

Family Perspectives

I was at Ted's feet, my head on his lap, dampening his gym pants with my tears. He stroked my cheek and said, in a jovial way, "Hey, aren't you supposed to be cheering me up?"

I looked up and brushed the tears away. The row of teddy bears on the shelf across from me smiled with encouragement. Ted's eyes flashed with mischief behind his rimless glasses. Funny, all of a sudden I *did* feel much better. I laughed. I'd been feeling so sorry for myself. Men problems, mother problems, moving problems – yes, I was moving again. Roz and Kathy had retired, and were coming over soon to begin renovations on their house. I only had three more weeks to find a place. I couldn't handle being close to the city, driving was difficult, and yet, I wanted to be close enough to go to Meditation and yoga classes as I knew they helped me so much. My mother was so critical of what I was going through that I hesitated to call her anymore. And of course, Art was not available to help me out and I knew the so-called relationship was ridiculous. There was no need to explain any of it. And really, in the big scheme of things, what did any of it matter?

I stood up and took my usual seat across from Ted, who was still sitting in his wheelchair in front of the TV I had turned off when I came in, and put on a Glenn Gould CD of Bach preludes instead, which we both enjoyed.

Feeling a little embarrassed, I asked, "Ted, do you have any suggestions for dealing with emotional issues? Praying and swearing hasn't worked for me."

Ted gazed at me and then said, "You know, I had a wonderful upbringing. My parents and twin sister gave me constant encouragement and support, even when I was too far away and too busy to have much contact with them. And my marriage was fairly even-keeled – apart from Charles' teenage shenanigans." He paused. "I have been thinking about Charles a lot lately. He and I were so different, and he was a very reactive child if he didn't get his way. In retrospect, though, I probably was lacking as a father – and as a husband, for that matter."

"Was your career taking most of your focus?"

"To put it mildly. Especially in the Yukon, where I was painting in a freer way than I had been trained. I wanted to devote all of my time to that, but teaching was a full-time job, which I thoroughly enjoyed. I loved those kids! Nicky was very patient and supportive, and I bet there were plenty of times she wished she could be doing something else. But, you know, it's fun to put myself into other people's shoes and imagine what they are experiencing."

"You mean you imagine having a rotten childhood or marriage?"

"Something like that – sure. It's good to use different scenarios. Not only does it make me more compassionate towards the average person, but it helps me be grateful for my own life and to downplay my own problems."

"Can you give me an example?" I asked, reaching for my notebook. "Why don't we write about Commitment or Marriage?"

My tears and worries had dissolved as they usually did in Ted's presence. He sat for a few seconds, looking regal despite his old checked brown shirt that had food stains on the front, and he began to speak.

Family Values

I love a fight and I get it with my family. The shrieks and groans, the shouts and screams make one believe they're at the doors of Hell and inside it *is* Hell.

My brother demands his selfish ways be met. My sister screams that her makeup has been displaced. She cannot find the lipstick, and the powder has disappeared. However, to me it matters not, because her face never looks any better. So, we live in this stew of familial turmoil.

What do the politicians mean when they wish us to return to family values? Do they mean return to constant embroilment and tiring arguments? I guess that underneath lies love, but love is so frightened that it hides under the table and rarely ventures out. And so, our family sails on choppy seas while outside sharks encircle our craft in the form of relatives. You cannot say that life is unexciting. There's enough drama to fill a dozen movies and a library full of books.

One could say the world is a stage, but the family is a theatre and every day the plot changes but the drama is ever-present. So, life becomes a theatre of drama and excitement. Luckily, there is no murder in the plot and we all live to have another battle next day.

"Ted," I said, when I was sure he was finished. "I love how you're able to sum up these 'poems' so that the last paragraph encapsulates the subject. I learn so much from you about writing, and trusting what wants to come out."

"I'm enjoying this," said Ted. "Do you mind if we do another one? Shall we do one on marriage since you've had two and I wouldn't be surprised if you have another? Frankly dear – it would be difficult to find the right person for you. You have so many interests, and the average man is going to make you feel guilty if you don't drop some of them for him. He would have to be creative also, and like what you create. If he didn't understand that side of you, you'd likely shut down. I'm sure you've had that happen before."

"I'm more apt to have done it to myself, Ted. It's in a woman's DNA to feel she's supposed to care for the man. And then she wonders why she feels resentful that her needs are put on the back burner. I bet your wife's life revolved around you."

"I can't say I'm proud of it. But we did have some jolly times and met wonderful people throughout the world. Are you ready to write? I want to experience a different life for a couple of minutes."

He rubbed his bristly head and looked surprised. "Do you like my new haircut?" He had already begun his poem before I could respond.

Marriage

I entered the church, more nervous than a mouse in Catland. All eyes turned as I stood at the altar and waited for the blushing bride to appear. The strains of the *Wedding March* heralded her coming and then followed the ceremony, sealed by a big fat kiss.

Afterwards, everybody drank their fill and gave out the cakes, and I was married. Two people facing God-knows-how-long together. Their fates sealed with signatures on paper and witnessed by the whole village. Then, we entered a life together.

Romance took a back seat to saving for a house and later, buying things for children to keep them happy. Gradually, we realized we had married strangers. The glow and intensity of the heat of courting and final capture gave way to the realization that love had grown cold. Each year added a block of ice to the chill until I was left living in a spiritual igloo. My unmarried friends had no signatures on their papers and were shacking up with abandon. Each girlfriend shone like a star for a couple of years and then was extinguished by brighter planets coming into view.

I quit the marriage scene after ten years and became a wandering star. It was a dark experience and I still float in the heavens of my thoughts. Marriage is a great and mountainous adventure but for some of us, the rope tatters, frays and breaks while climbing the heights, and we are left dangling in the voids of life's precipices.

Oh, that love was not so fragile. It's akin to walking across an icy pond carrying high quality porcelain. While the cups are whole, let us enjoy the beverage of marriage and keep the crockery from cracking.

"Ted, I love the imagery. It just pours out of you, without a pause. Brilliant!"

"Oh, Pet, you're my Muse on this. I'm really enjoying our little project."

"The pleasure is all mine."

"You know what I've been dreaming about lately?"

I laughed. "You mean, really dreaming, or imagining?"

"Who knows – I do spend a lot of time sleeping. But I have been thinking a lot about Germany. Would you like to go on a cruise with me? I'm sure you would love the architecture, and the art and music. I want to see it again before I die, and I want to see how much of the language I remember."

"We might need to bring along a nurse, Ted. I'm not putting baby powder on your bottom."

Ted roared with laughter, and just then, Glenn Gould's tones built to a stunning climax. We sat together, enjoying the piano tones, and imagining a cruise up the Rhine.

Memories

I watched Ted sleeping in front of the TV. The show was of two chefs concocting food and making jokes. Once, Ted would have enjoyed it but he was despondent about most things now. This place was not at all stimulating for him.

Ted rarely had visitors, partly because his guardians protected him from people that would exhaust him, and partly because it was often difficult to communicate with him. Plus, if Ted was bored with someone, he didn't hide it. Most people assumed he had gotten much deafer than he used to be. I had figured out that he just needed the batteries in his hearing aids changed.

Ted was in his wheelchair, his head pulled down and forward on his chest, his skin extremely pale but glowing with health, and his glasses falling down his nose. His comfy chair was still facing the wall.

I figured I might as well leave. I was still very depressed myself with my continuing problems with electromagnetic sensitivity. My mother had died in Ontario, and I was unable to be there for her or help my sister and brother. My mother had been angry when I wouldn't come home to help her in the last stages of her life but I was too ill to fly. Being a Christian Scientist, she didn't understand my fear. As it was, I still needed to sleep in my special tent that acted like a faraday cage to give some reprieve from all that I felt. I hadn't been downtown in months and just coming here was exhausting. But I knew my anxiety was improving and visiting Ted for a short time could lift both of our spirits.

The door opened and a large woman with a heavy Russian accent said, "Oh 'Scuse – I come back."

Ted looked up and managed a smile when he saw me. I motioned to the woman to come back. "Hello, I'm Jan. Would you mind checking Ted's hearing aids?" I asked.

While she looked for batteries, Ted said, "I was just dreaming about you. Perhaps, I could sense you were here."

"Wonderful to see you, Ted," I said, giving him a hug.

The woman took Ted's hearing aids out and quickly popped in new batteries.

"How often do you do that?" I asked her.

"About once a week. When people ask," she replied.

She left and Ted said, "You look tired, dear."

"I can't seem to sleep very well," I said.

"Hah – that's about all I do. What would I do without my dreams? It seems like ages since I've seen you."

"It has been at least a couple of weeks, Ted," I said. I turned off the TV. "I moved again."

"Again?"

"This is a little more permanent. I'm renting a cabin in the woods. It's only six hundred square feet but I've squeezed in my necessities, and it's rather nice to get rid of things and simplify." I still hadn't told Ted anything about my condition. Even my best friends didn't believe my problem, although there was more and more information about it online. And as a neurologist I saw said, 'how can we keep increasing the number of cell towers, satellites and hand-held devices, and assume that our bodies can handle it. Far more people are suffering than we're hearing about.' I still was only teaching a handful of students, and rarely played a gig. I was grateful for the inheritance from my parents which was allowing me to try new remedies as I sought freedom from discomfort. Other people in my condition were not nearly so lucky.

I looked over at the top of the bookshelf and saw a photo I hadn't seen before. It was of Ted with several people on the steps of a cabin. "Is that your cabin at Carcross?"

"Yes, a friend just sent it to me. We had such a good time there."

"There's something about being close to nature that puts everyone in a good mood. Some of my best memories are of

162

holidays on lakes and oceans. Did you have lots of people for meals there?"

"Mostly potlucks, as I recall. We had wonderful conversations around our dinner table. That's what I miss the most here. There's no dinner conversation."

"I know, Ted. This situation is tragic. I know you love dinner parties as much as I do. I won't be able to entertain a gang in my renovated garage."

"I bet it's charming. I'd like to see it."

"I hope you will," I said, but knew it would be impossible to take him out now. He was dependent on the machines that were used to get him in and out of chairs.

I looked at the photograph again. "Ted, did I tell you I took part in a special weekend workshop in Nanaimo and the Chief of Carcross was attending?"

"Mark?"

"Yes, I just ran across his card. Mark Wedge."

"I remember when he was small. A very intelligent lad."

"He's still pretty small but he must be at least my age. I went with Artie to take the Pursuit of Excellence Course, which is all about communication, and Mark was there to see if it would be helpful for his clan. He was surprised by how much that program had to offer. We had to act out different scenarios. We chose each other as partners because we seemed to be the most outgoing there. You know, not afraid of getting up in front of people. We went for lunch to discuss our approach but instead we had a wonderful conversation."

"Did he tell you about his family?"

"He told me that when he was very small, he went out with some of the men in canoes to go hunting. They told him to turn his head so he wouldn't see them harpooning animals. While he was sitting in the back of the canoe, he saw a beaver with two tails swim under the canoe. When he told the men, they told him he would be the next chief because that was the sign."

"I'm not sure Mark was keen on being a chief."

"He shared that he wanted to keep his spiritual beliefs to himself but he felt such pressure, even by his partner, to be more open with the clan. Actually, I found him to be very open about everything we discussed."

Ted sat straighter in his chair and sipped some water through a straw. I opened the blind so that he could see the tree on Shelbourne Street. "Hey, Ted, let's go for a walk. The sun is shining and you could do with some fresh air."

"I don't think so, dear. It looks cold out there. I was just thinking about how it's so wonderful that you continue to visit me, and then I remembered different people I used to visit when I was younger."

"It's not cold outside, Ted, but if you like, we can try writing something down instead?"

Memories

I love sitting with older people because they have many, many memories. Although their bodies are bent with age and their hands have a tremor, which they endeavour to control, inside their heads are beautiful visions of the golden days of youth when they loved and were loved – when they played and had energy, which was inexhaustible. Although many of them are in their 90s, they remember their mothers calling them and the bright cries of their siblings which echo through the years.

History is constantly repeated in the mind and it is very precious because it is unique. My grandfather could remember the Boer war and my grandmother's sister married George Stevenson who invented the rocket, which was the first railway engine. I remember hunting for crabs on the beach and finding big ones, which we cooked over a stove heated by sea coal washed up on the beaches.

Life had no worries for we children but many for our parents. They protected us from reality so we never realized the true tragedy of everyday life – lack of money, shortage of food and no luxuries. The memories of sunny days and playing on the hills amidst the flowers are what remain.

Children no longer enjoy nature as we did. They are imprisoned by television and gadgets, which may nourish the intellect but not the soul. Leave me with my old memories.

Primrose banks full of flowers and wandering over the hill to see the little farmhouse at its base. Then, home to my mother's greeting and hot plain meals – the memories of which still come to me as I sit and meditate.

I put the journal aside and watched Ted sitting calmly. He never moved a muscle when he was relaxing. I felt like I was often rubbing my hands or tapping my foot, or making some kind of a movement but Ted didn't seem to have any nervous energy.

I saw a pile of postcards beside his bed. I started going through them. "Ted, where did these come from? They're wonderful." Each card was one of Ted's paintings obviously copied by a child and on the back were questions to Ted about his artwork. I started reading some of them out loud. "Dear Mr. Harrison, I love your colours. And the pictures are happy. How do you come up with your ideas? Dear Mr. Harrison, thank you for inspiring our classroom. Why did you paint the whale pink? Dear Mr. Harrison, my Mom said you're famous but you don't act like it. Do you have a limo? Dear Mr. Harrison, did you always want to be an artist?"

Ted interrupted me. "I have to answer those. Can you help me?"

"Of course, Ted, but do you know where they came from or how we can figure out what school they're from? There isn't an envelope so someone must have come by with them. Were you out visiting a school lately?"

"I don't think I've been out in a while," said Ted.

I looked at the guest book. If it was accurate, no one had visited him in two weeks. No wonder he was depressed.

"Ted, that settles it, I'm taking you outside. Now that you have this new wheelchair, it's much easier for me to push so let's get you cozy and we'll look at the world. And we'll have a coffee while we're out. That'll keep you awake."

Although Ted grumbled, with the help of an aide, we were soon in the sunshine making our way up the quiet road behind Shelbourne Street. Our first stop was at the house with the old yellow dog that was always lying in the driveway. But this time he wasn't there. "He's probably passed on, the lucky dog," said Ted.

"Ted, he might be inside."

"No, not on a day like today. I must say, I am glad to be out here. It's so beautiful. I think I should buy one of these little houses. That's all I need." I smiled. Ted didn't have access to any money and I tried to picture what he would buy if he did.

I decided to walk the four blocks to the park with large Garry oaks, a playground and an asphalt path around it. Ted would be happy to see some children. We had gone a couple of blocks when we saw a woman coming towards us, dressed in glittery clothes and carrying two puppies. I slowed down and said to her, "Wow – you look wonderful. Are you performing somewhere?"

She smiled and said, "No, I just like bling and wear it all the time."

"Isn't she beautiful, Ted?"

"I'll say," said Ted, eyeing her sequinned blue jeans and silvery short top that left her midriff bare. She had a ring on every finger and several sparkly earrings in each ear.

I turned to her and said, "Would you mind putting a puppy in Ted's lap? He loves dogs and doesn't get to see one very often."

She was more than willing to oblige and soon, Ted had bonded with the affectionate puppy, Cornelius. With regrets, he handed the puppy back to the vivacious woman and we were on our way again. After a bit, Ted said, "Did you see that ruby in her belly button?"

I laughed. "I guess your view was lower than mine. Wouldn't you think that would be uncomfortable?"

"She loves her glitter – and her dogs," said Ted. "Maybe she finds two is a bit much for her. I could take on Cornelius."

Once we were at the park, I placed Ted beside a baby who was smiling contentedly in a buggy. I sat on a swing beside the parents of the child who were proudly watching their little girl interact with Ted. Ted was lifting his eyebrows and pulling faces for her. I told the parents, who looked like they were East Indian, that Ted was an artist.

Two boys aged ten or eleven were playing on the monkey bars beside us but they ran over to Ted. "Mr. Harrison, we thought that was you. You came to our school. You were so rad. Can we have a picture of you?" They crouched beside him and did a selfie of the three of them. I had to laugh, watching these youngsters with their cell phones. I wondered if I would ever be able to handle having one. I got the name of their school, in case that was the one that dropped off the post cards, but they said Ted's visit had been two years before.

Ted seemed to become more and more alert as he chatted to the boys, and the parents of the child. Then, he leaned his head back and stared at the huge trees. The sun was filtering through the thick leaves, and once again, I was grateful to whoever saved the parkland in Victoria.

We resumed our walk, taking another street back, stopping to look at different gardens, and eventually, coming to the Mall. "Ted, would you like ice cream or coffee."

"I'd like a cone, please."

As we came to the door at the Dairy Queen, a couple of people rushed to open it for Ted's wheelchair. Even if they didn't know who Ted was, they seemed to be curious as they watched him lick his cone with concentration, unable to keep up to the drips. When I went over to tidy his hands, Ted said, "I know I'm sloppy but leave me be. It's such a treat."

As we made our way back to Parkwood, Ted asked me to stop. "Look at those clouds. I don't think we usually have clouds like that."

I didn't tell him that I thought they were chem trails. I had once heard Ted make a mention of them in one of his poems, but there was no point in discussing that. Because of my sensitivity, I was on the alert about anything out of the ordinary. But these clouds, although they were beautiful, did not strike me as the least bit normal. The American military base on Whidbey Island a few miles away was a little too close to ignore. The growlers could be heard constantly from my cabin, which was close to the ocean. I even wondered about all the submarine activity in our area. Naval Base Kitsap, located on the eastern shore of Hood Canal – less than twenty miles away – is home port for eight of the U.S. Navy's fourteen Trident ballistic missile submarines and an underground nuclear weapons storage complex. Together, they're believed to store more than 1,300 nuclear warheads. This is arguably the biggest single concentration of nuclear warheads in the world. Because I didn't know what had caused my sensitivity, I often wondered if this could be part of it. I had suggested it to the Neurologist and he said he knew that they were getting into using electromagnetic pulses in their warfare, so anything was possible.

Once Ted was back in his room, he suggested we write about the sky.

Clouds

Whenever I am bored, I look to the sky and there before me is a great panoply of clouds. They have infinite shapes and infinite colours. Fat fleecy clouds float slowly across my vision. Sometimes they grow angry and their plump shapes darken, presaging rain or storm, often accompanied by an aerial show of lightning and a booming sound effect of thunder, which drones across the sky adding a musical score to the vast show.

The sky is made interesting by the varied formations of cloud. They mirror our lives, which often have cloudy periods and a few storms. However, just as the sky is made more interesting by these formations, so are our lives, which intermingle both cloud and sunshine. The thing about clouds is they disintegrate after changing their shapes. The sun comes out and in no time, the sky is clear – a blank canvas tinted blue waiting for the next families of clouds to appear on the stage. Before nightfall, they glow in a brilliant finale of late sunshine before darkness envelops the whole scene.

I was feeling agitated from being in an area with so many businesses and wanted to get back to my funny little cabin in the woods, and perhaps have a nap in my 'tent'. Maybe Ted was ready for a nap too.

"Shall I buzz someone and get them to put you to bed for a nap before dinner?"

"No need for that. Find me something to watch on the telly. I wish we could have dinner at Ken's but I don't think I could manage that."

I put on a show about jungle birds and plants, and watched for a short time beside him, before I slipped out the door.

Bowls and Bells

I closed the door of Ted's room and set the padded gold bag down beside the hospital bed. Ted was sitting in his wheelchair, staring out the window at the few branches and leaves of the tree he could see. It was a rather dull day but at least it wasn't raining. Cartoons flickered on the muted TV. Ted was facing the opposite direction, lost in thought, and hadn't heard me come in.

I put my hand on his shoulder and he almost managed a smile when he turned his head. "Oh, it's you. Do you know that I'm the only one in this huge house?"

"Where is everyone?" I was mystified. I had passed the usual group that sat on chairs outside his room, and he would be going to the dining room for meals.

"I have no idea. It's certainly weird."

I didn't reply but sat thinking about how Ted and I seemed to be following a similar arc when it came to our brains. He was alone here with his imagination and in his depressed state, perhaps, he was picturing calamity. But I was determined to beat my problems and I knew Ted would have done the same if he was physically able to join me on some of my unusual searches. I had recently spent a week at the Biocybernaut Institute with my brain hooked up by electrodes to computers so that I was able to listen to my brain waves and train them to go from Beta to Alpha. My depression had lifted and I was excited about my future. I was able to meditate with ease. There are scientific studies that showed this kind of training is equal to 20 to 40 years of Zen meditation, increasing the I.Q. by eleven points and creativity by 50%. It also reverses brain aging which Ted would have loved to try. Ted was in no state to hear such a story. His curiosity was replaced with frustration and unhappiness.

Just then, a slim, blonde woman in her forties walked in and cheerfully said, "Hello, folks, I'm just cleaning the bathroom. I won't be long."

We could smell the bleach and hear her singing an Adelle song: *Never mind I'll find someone like you. I wish nothing but the best for you.* Her tone was lovely. I refrained from putting a CD on so that we could listen to her. Ted seemed interested and lifted his eyebrows at me when she held the last note with perfect pitch and a natural vibrato.

When she came out, I said, "Hey, you've got a beautiful voice. Thanks for that."

She removed her iPod plugs and laughed. "I don't even know I'm doing it but music sure helps the day slide by."

"I agree. By the way, Ted was wondering if there are fewer people around these days."

"Here? Are you kidding? We're choc-a-block. It's noisy out there. Ted's smart to keep his door shut. It's nice we don't have to lock it anymore. The woman that kept walking into rooms isn't here anymore. Well," she said, swinging her bucket around and putting her plugs back in. "Enjoy your visit."

Once the door was closed, I said, "I guess you aren't the only one here after all, Ted."

"Maybe not," he said, rubbing his bristly head. "I just wish I could move on. I'm so tired of this."

"I know, Ted. You're so ready." I gave him a big hug.

He stared into my eyes and finally smiled. "Have you been teaching?"

"Not today. I was playing at the Esquimalt United church this morning. And I saw Ken. He's opening a coffee shop beside his restaurant and he was in there working on it when I walked back to my car. I knocked on the window and he invited me in for a visit."

"My Ken? Did you ask him why he never visits me anymore? Is he disappointed in me, that I never did the mural?"

"Of course, not. Ken and Shelly, and baby Ted adore you. But Ken was upset about not being told you had moved. And then when he tracked you down, he was told he wasn't on the list of people that were allowed to see you."

"What list? Why don't I have a say in any of this? Who is doing this to me?"

"They probably think they're doing you a service but the loneliness must be unbearable. You are so strong, Ted."

"Yeah, well sometimes I wish I weren't."

"Anyway, I gave Ken my card so we can stay in touch. He also wants Ted to take piano lessons from me, apparently."

"That's a wonderful idea. I like picturing that."

I bent down and unzipped the bag.

"What's that you've got?"

"It's my latest instrument. It's a crystal singing bowl that is used for sound therapy. This particular one has anchi crystals in it that are over a billion years old. I played this today for the congregation at church during meditation and they were so interested in it, I thought you might like it. We all sang 'Dona Nobis Pacem' with its sound."

I removed the bubble wrap and held up the large purple crystal bowl. Balancing it on my left hand, I used a suede covered mallet to strike it and get it ringing, and then I ran the mallet around the rim to increase the volume and duration. I sang '*Nam Myoho Renge Kyo*' as a chant. Ted's mouth was open as he watched me.

The beautiful resonance slowly disappeared. "I've never heard anything like it."

"Here, Ted. Let me put it in your lap so you can feel the vibrations."

Ted didn't move a muscle as I repeated the experiment with it sitting on his lap. "Jan, I love that. Thank you. How did you find it?"

"Something made me Google crystal bowls and it turned out there's a woman in town who brings them in to sell, from Salt Lake City. She only lives a few blocks from me so the next day, I went over to her place and she let me try several. You can get different types of crystals embedded in them and they all have different healing qualities. This one is supposed to unite and harmonize the energy field, and give a natural connection to the higher self. In other words, it makes you feel fantastic."

"Yes, it does. Do it again please."

Ted closed his eyes as the vibrations moved through and around him.

"What are you singing?"

"It's a chant that is part of the daily Buddhist practice. It's something about the law of cause and effect through sound. These bowls make me want to add more sound to them. Vocal sounds are amplified by the bowl's vibrations. We chant things like this in kundalini yoga classes and I find them to be very powerful. They help to relax and they increase energy."

"That bowl makes me think of the bells pealing in our village church on Sundays. Perhaps, we should write a poem about it."

I was surprised. Ted hadn't thought about writing poems in months and I no longer suggested it. In fact, of late, he didn't seem to know what I meant when I mentioned the poems. I found something to write on from his table of papers and soon, he was speaking in the relaxed easy way that I hadn't heard in a while. I wondered if the bowl really did have healing qualities.

Bells

It was said by the ancient Greeks that when the temple bells cease to ring, the flowers ring with their heads waving in the wind and the voice of the bell emanating from the flower.

Bells have always been thought of as magical. They can be happy, and peal loudly and vigorously, or they can be sad and peel slowly and ponderously. Through the last war in Britain, all church bells ceased to ring because if their voice was heard, it was either an invasion by the enemy or some special tragedy that had befallen the nation. When Peacetime came, they broke out into a cacophony of joy. They were in tune with the spirit of the people who were thankful that the period of stress was over and they could know that the bells were just there to call people to worship as they had been for centuries.

The bells reflected the mood of the whole nation and were happy to ring again once more in peace. The great sound of wedding bells signal that love has conquered and the blushing bride goes to the church with the joyful bells ringing in her ears. They are the same bells which will call people to the funeral of the bride or groom sometime in their lives.

We learn to listen to the messages of the bells. Like Quasi Modo, the Hunchback of Notre Dame, who rang the bells in the Cathedral, and his poor misshapen body gave a message of happiness and hope to the people of Paris.

Nowadays, we have to listen carefully because bells are not rung so frequently as they were. There are other noises that fill the air like car horns, hooters, and unmusical sounds which pervade the atmosphere.

Let us feel joy when we can still hear a bell, either in unison with others or solitary, giving a message of both happiness and hope to the world. In the rush of modern life, other sounds have taken their place but there is nothing quite like the sound of a bell from an isolated church in the countryside speaking to us personally and accompanying the voices of songbirds. Nature and bells in unison.

The nurse's aide came in to say that she would be back in a few minutes to take him to dinner, but Ted was not ready to give up an opportunity for a conversation, which he had been without for too long. And he also didn't miss much when it came to my feelings. As he spoke about church bells, I was wondering if I'd ever be well enough to have a normal relationship with a man. I was still handicapped with my sensitivity and had to limit venturing out for long. Today had been a long day for me.

"Jan, I'm just wondering if you feel you have friends you can go to. Living alone can be difficult."

"Thanks for worrying about me, Ted. Yes, I have lots of friends." I remembered how when I had pneumonia and a nose that was gushing blood from a burst artery a few months previously, there wasn't anyone I felt I wanted to bother to take me to the hospital. I drove myself to emergency with a blood-soaked towel held to my face. It wasn't that I didn't feel my friends would help me. It was more that I was afraid of bothering people. Or maybe I was overly independent. Or my depression made me feel unworthy. But thanks to all the unconventional therapies I had tried during the last year, I was feeling so much happier.

"Friendship is a complicated business," said Ted, as he watched the thoughts flicker across my face. "Let's write about it. I'm not hungry anyway."

Friends

You know a friend when you have one. Old friends are like diamonds – precious and rare. New friends are like autumn leaves – found everywhere (or so my mother said). When you have a friend you can trust, you are very fortunate – one that can perhaps hold a secret. A friend will keep that secret, but someone who isn't a friend will blab it around just to make his or her life a little more exciting.

Some friends are so good that you can share your life with them. You can take them on holidays and allow them to take you on holidays, which is the perfect thing. However, to keep the pot of friendship warm, you have to keep in touch with them.

I personally have had many good friends who I'm out of touch with now, so the friendship is no longer close. You can have girlfriends, boyfriends, little friends, big friends – they come in all shapes, sizes and ages. There's nothing better than to meet a friend after many years of separation and the joy one feels overcomes the lost times that you could have had together.

A great source of a secure friendship is to have served in the Military. Your friends are your comrades as you undergo the rigors of military life, heated and warmed by a shared experience, which can be harsh. It is the unity of friendship in the forces which make a military friend so dear to you. Even years later, you remember how you faced life together, and now they've disappeared from your world because of time and distance. In war, you have enemies on the other side that could be real friends if you were not in this artificial circumstance. Ex-enemies can prove to be the best of friends once the struggle is over and everything has settled down into a normal existence.

An African once put it to me. He said, 'Why were your enemies the Germans when they are like you – white and Christian – and Jesus said you have to love your neighbor – so why did you fight each other?' I found it hard to answer him because it was quite true. We *were* both supposed to follow the teachings of Christianity and yet, we didn't because our national policy was to remain as enemies. So, politicians, in order to divert the attention of those ruled by them, can create a state of hatred, which appeals to only a few in the community and yet has long-lived repercussions. In a war, you cannot love your enemies and they cannot love you because hatred is the gasoline that drives the motor.

However, in a polite society such as ours, we can all be friends because friendship is the glue that holds the community and the nation together. And friendship too should hold a marriage together. But this often fails because of selfishness on either side where we allow our wants to become superior to the wants of our partners.

So, true friendship calls for a sacrifice on both sides. The sacrifice is that you often give way to your friend's needs instead of what yours are. But this has to be mutual.

David and Jonathan were lovely in their lives, and in their deaths, they were not divided. This great biblical friendship rings out over the centuries. We are all very fortunate to have a good friend. It makes life so much better, but requires understanding and knowledge to keep it going.

I sat with the paper on my lap thinking about all the things I was afraid of, yet, all the things that bothered me were created by people that could potentially be my friends. What a strange world we lived in.

Ted sat watching me with the Buddha-like smile on his lips. I was so grateful for the love I felt from this beautiful man. If only I could help him. I knew that it was only selfishness that kept me from praying that he could move on. He was so unhappy in this situation. But the thought of never being able to spend time with him was beyond thinking of. An aide came in to take Ted to dinner and neither one of us spoke. He just blew me a kiss and I did my best to smile with assurance.

The Last Supper

I was visiting Ted for the last time, and despite my grief, I was very happy for him. He had been miserable for the last two years in this place. Mary, the head nurse in the building, had explained to me the previous day that he was not being given any treatment for pneumonia, and he wouldn't be given any sustenance. It was just a matter of time. My father had gone through a similar experience two years earlier.

In my father's case, I had been angry to see his long, strong body be reduced to a skeleton. I felt we should find a way to speed up the process. But the few times he regained consciousness, I saw a look of wonder and bliss in his eyes that I'd never seen before, and I came to realize he needed to go through his own personal process. The tough Scotsman was opening his heart perhaps. He even wept when the chaplain played a traditional lullaby on his Scottish flute.

In contrast, Ted's heart had been open most of his life. Mary had tears in her eyes as she shared her feelings for this special man. As she spoke, I stood and watched Ted lying unconscious in the bed, and I hoped that it would be a quick transition for him.

I was scheduled to fly out of Victoria the following day to visit Artie in Cambodia. He was trying to find a place where he could afford to take early retirement and while in Sihanoukville, he had gotten very sick. He had phoned the day before and convinced me I needed to come there. I knew this must be serious because he was fiercely independent and rarely asked anyone for help. I had agreed despite my sensitivities. Art was a friend I would always be connected to. I couldn't leave before I said good-bye to Ted, though. Since this was my last chance to be with him, I was going to spend the day in his room.

I had a knapsack of things to occupy myself: Ted's portfolio of poems, crossword puzzles, snacks, a thermos of green tea, and a couple of ciders. I passed some of the agitated and unhappy residents that were sitting in the hallway outside Ted's room and was glad that I wouldn't have to see this again. Although – who knew? – perhaps, I would be the next one living here.

When I came in, the room was different. Everything was tidy, the TV was off and soft music was playing. The lights were dim and the curtains were pulled. Ted still looked the same with his lovely round face and serene expression, his hands folded across his chest. The row of teddy bears looked more solemn than usual as they held their vigil.

I opened the folder of poems. One I hadn't read in a long time was at the top. It was dated January 26/09, almost exactly six years previously.

Ted Harrison's Mind Travels

I was sitting drinking tea. It was green tea and tasted very, very smooth. When suddenly, the world as I knew it ended, and I with it. So, I never ever drank the whole cup because the rays emanating from outer space destroyed all human life on earth but left the buildings made by man. The trees still grew and the flowers continued to bloom with all their beauty, but there was no mankind to admire them. Nature carried on and did not even shed a tear for the passing of humanity.

The only sounds left in the world were natural ones. No car engines throbbing, no airplanes flying, no noise of industry and no pollution from that. The earth returned to its primitive, pristine state and with the disappearance of mankind, God disappeared. Churches were empty and would never be filled again. Yet, birds still sang, and the hillside gleamed in the sun and flourished as never before.

The earth had not died with the passing of humanity. It stayed as it always has done – hurtling along in space – and after years and years of travel, the hand of man could no longer be discerned. It was as if humanity had never been. And the moldering leaves of history decayed or were blown away by the wind. Our monument was a blank sheet.

The rule of nature took over, leaving the birds and beasts as kings and queens.

I smiled as I read the last line. This was a great example of how blasé Ted was about human life and how much respect he had for the power of nature. I put the folder aside and leaned over Ted. Resting my hands lightly on his chest, I said, "Ted, you are loved all around the world."

I gasped when Ted opened his eyes and said, "Where did you fly in from? Sit me up."

With joy, I raised the end of the bed so that he could look around and I found him his glasses. I couldn't find his hearing aids but we were communicating with our eyes and our clasped hands.

"Are you having a cider?" he asked.

I pulled one out and offered it to him but he said, "What else have you got?"

I held up one of his favourite yogurt suckers he'd fancied of late. His eyes lit up and he was soon sucking on an orange one. "What a delicious lolly," he said. He hadn't eaten in several days so he seemed to be devouring this. For the next ten minutes, he didn't say anything except how super-dupe it was. When it was finished, he said, "Shouldn't we be watching a movie?"

I found the channel with subtitles and there was Audrey Hepburn's *Breakfast at Tiffany's*.

"Oh good – let's watch this. What else do you have to eat?" asked Ted.

"I'm just going to go out and ask what they think is best for you, Ted. I'll be right back."

It was quite a coincidence to find the nurse and Ted's favourite dining assistant – the jolly, small man from Nepal – conferring together outside Ted's door. Usually, it was difficult to track the nurse down without a long wait, as she was so busy with a large unit of unhealthy residents. "Oh, hello," I said. "Listen, Ted is really hungry and I'm wondering what you think he should have."

They looked at me with open mouths and both said at the same time, "Ted?"

"Yes," I said, unable to stop grinning. "And you know I think he's ready to party, so the more interesting it is for him the better. I have some cashews and chocolates but I'm not sure that's such a good idea." Their eyes were sparkling as they looked at each other and laughed.

The nurse told the assistant what to get and he rushed off to the kitchen. She followed me into Ted's room. "Ted, how are you feeling?" she asked.

Ted frowned at her as he tried to read her lips. She felt his forehead but didn't try to take his blood pressure. "I love this movie," said Ted. Just then, the Nepalese man came in and joked with Ted as he gave him some liquid food to drink with a straw. Ted smiled back at him before sucking noisily. They left after a short time.

We watched the rest of the movie with me sipping cider and Ted drinking his dinner. Ted looked over at me and said, "I'm so glad you're having a cider." He squeezed my hand and I wondered if he knew this was a last supper for us.

Ted's eyes were heavy and I leaned over to speak in his ear. "Ted, I'm going to Asia tomorrow. Are you going to be okay by yourself here?"

"Of course, Dear. Don't worry about anything."

I put the bed in a prone position and watched Ted fall asleep. As I sat there, holding space for Ted, I looked out the window and could see the moon partially peeking out from a cloud. I returned to the folder of poems and found another one Ted had written about the moon.

The Moon

She hid her face behind a cloud tonight – my friend, the moon. Every night I look for her and she looks for me, and we find each other on the balcony. Then, her face appears as the cloud dissipates. What a joy to see her smiling down, making the night beautiful. She's wearing her best tonight. I can see the glittering stars circling around her.

Oh, and there is Venus – the brightest star of all. The star of love. The star which welcomes the human eye. If distance lends enchantment, we have it here. The moon is so remote and yet, so near, and Venus is even remoter. It takes us weeks to journey there. However, earthbound as we are, we must watch and admire from afar like some rare princess or queen we're not allowed to touch. We can just gaze in awe and feel enriched by her presence. She has been hovering there for millions of years and in the fraction of time we live, she has enriched the darkest night.

Let us be glad that we can see her and enjoy the ethereal vision of star and moon. The symbols of Islam – what a beautiful thought.

Three days later, I woke up in Sihanoukville to the news that Ted Harrison had passed on. Several of my friends had emailed and I watched the report by CBC. I felt a confused sadness and joy as I read on my iPad what several newspapers had to say about Ted. Barry told me that Ted had never regained consciousness after my visit with him.

When I had arrived in Sihanoukville, I had found Artie shivering with cold but burning up. He refused to let me take him to the hospital, saying he didn't want to die in such a place. I put my long underwear on him and placed my winter coat over the thin blanket. Turning the air conditioning off, I opened the windows and felt agitated as I tried to block the cacophony outside. Dogs barked, motors roared, people laughed in the courtyard below, music throbbed on the beach blocks away, roosters crowed and salesmen bartered. I interrupted Artie's feverish dreams to urge him to drink coconut water and soda. The previous night, Artie's high fever had finally broken. We hadn't left his stuffy room in two days and as he watched me quietly weeping as I read the emails, he said, "I'm going to take you to a remote beach so you can have a swim. We'll take a bit of picnic. I'm starving."

Without enthusiasm, I climbed into his old Renault and held on for dear life as he dealt with the way people drove on the war-torn roads in that country, ignoring red lights and passing on two-laned highways, despite trucks bearing down from the other direction. The car had no air conditioning and the windows wouldn't open so I wondered if we would die of asphyxiation or from a wild accident. The more I watched though, I could see that people were very aware of each other as they broke all the rules. There seemed to be a harmonious rhythm involved. I remembered someone mentioning that Buddhists were much better drivers because they saw each other as part of themselves, rather than separate entities.

True to his word, we came to a beautiful, private, white sandy beach where turquoise water lapped the shore. Artie pulled out the cooler and a couple of chairs to put under a palm tree, and I ran down and dove into the water. I lay on my back and let my sorrow flow, the tears joining the salty warm water. Then, I heard Ted's voice. "Don't be sad, dear. I'm so happy to be in this beautiful place. I love you."

I continued to float on the surface and looked at the sky, expecting to see Ted flying above me, wearing a lumberjack checked shirt and jeans. Maybe he would be riding on a motorcycle. Or maybe he would just be sitting on a cloud waving and blowing kisses. The more I relaxed and thought about Ted, and the voice I was sure I had heard, the happier I became.

I swam to shore and ran up to join Artie. He handed me a cold cider and said, "You're looking much better. I knew you needed a swim."

"Artie – Ted did a fly-by. He's okay." I couldn't stop smiling.

Artie clinked his bottle against mine, kissed me, and said, "What the Bleep do we know, eh?" He was referring to the quantum physics movie he insisted I watch with him a few years before.

When we came back to the guest house, I checked my messages and read a new email from Barry. He said that he had woken up that day and there was a huge gorgeous moose in his front field, which was very rare, and the morning sky was a beautiful mauve. Barry said he knew it was our pal saying he's fine. I shook my head and grinned. Barry had had his own sign from Ted.

I thought about my amazing last visit in Victoria with Ted. I decided Ted did that for me so that I would remember him as I always will – with a sparkle in his eye, a zest for life, and a big open heart. My beautiful teacher, my beautiful friend.